Elizabeth Hazard

Autumn musings

and other poems

Elizabeth Hazard

Autumn musings
and other poems

ISBN/EAN: 9783337374754

Printed in Europe, USA, Canada, Australia, Japan

Cover: Foto ©Thomas Meinert / pixelio.de

More available books at **www.hansebooks.com**

AND

OTHER POEMS.

BY

ELIZABETH HAZARD.

PHILADELPHIA:
J. B. LIPPINCOTT & CO.
1874.

TO .

ROWLAND G. HAZARD

THESE POEMS

ARE AFFECTIONATELY INSCRIBED

BY HIS SISTER,

THE AUTHOR.

CONTENTS.

POEMS.

AUTUMN MUSINGS.

When soft the mist upon the mountain lies,
And soft the light descends from golden skies;
When woods and lawns and hills their mirror make
In the calm surface of the sleeping lake,
And in its depth serene as clearly show
As though their real forms were there below;
When a deep silence reigns throughout the air,
And nature seems the pensive thought to share
That the expiring year hastes to its close,
Disrob'd and cheerless as from thence it rose;
When hoary winter held his icy reign,
And cold and cheerless lay the frozen plain,
And bare and leafless wav'd the forest-trees
To the low moaning of the gusty breeze,
Or sway'd their clashing branches to the blast
As in its might the wasting tempest pass'd,
Low laying many a monarch of the wood
That there in pride for centuries had stood,
And felt with genial spring's advancing glow
The sap ascending through its vessels flow,
Till rife with life each bright'ning twig was seen
To ope its buds and don its robe of green;

Their color deep'ning still from day to day,
Till thick'ning shades obscured the solar ray,
And grateful coolness round in summer spread
From leafy bowers of graceful form o'erhead,
Infusing in the soul that dreamy trance
That sees Titania lead her fairy dance
Round the small circle in the flow'ry mead,
And Oberon's mailed knights in armor tread;
Or teach the heart with mystic lore to glow,
Till forth the legendary tale doth flow,
And the creations of the mind have place
With life's realities among our race.
In caverns deep see superstitious forms
Hold converse with the rulers of the storms,
And call the winged lightning from the cloud,
Or day's fair face with night's mantle shroud,
Mutt'ring enchantments, till, by Genii's spell,
Kings great and brave submissive to them dwell,
And at the breathing of a charmed word
The elements above, beneath, are stirr'd,
And spirits haste their bidding to obey
In darkness of the night or splendor of the day,
Till, with the sun's decreasing heat and glow,
The sap had ceased its vivifying flow,
And summer dreams had fled before the reign
Of golden autumn's pow'r o'er wood and plain,
And, russet turn'd, from many a lofty tree
Its beauteous garniture fell suddenly.
A chilling blast upon the wings of night
Pass'd by, and when the morning light
Uprose with gladd'ning beam so bright and clear,
Its beauty was effaced, its foliage sere;

But not before the task that spring propos'd
In germinating buds was seal'd and clos'd,
Which the forthcoming year shall fresh unfold
From the protecting cerements, round them roll'd,
To wave in beauty 'neath the summer skies
When odors rich from lovely flow'rs arise.

So in the vig'rous years of manhood's pride,
When life seems flowing in its fullest tide,
Disease insidious cometh oft unseen,
And of its lustre strips the loftiest mien,
Lays its fair beauty perished in the dust,
And wastes the props of earthly hope and trust;
But virtue's germs that drank the dew of heav'n,
For their maturing that was freely giv'n,
Immortal with the soul shall then arise
In fullness to expand in Paradise.

Some as the hectic hue on maiden's brow,
Where slow, consuming sickness spreads its glow
And lights a fearful lustre in the eyes,
The altar-flame of a pure sacrifice,
With fitful beam alternate pales and burns,
Now dims and now with brighter glow returns,
Till the last vital spark's extinguish'd ray
Sinks in th' advancing gloom of dark decay,
And, as a meteor on the brow of night
Expiring, sheds its gleam of brightest light,
With lovelier hues their glowing charms disclose
When healthful life no longer through them flows.

Some as gay flow'rs their touch'd foliage wreathes
Round fragile shrubs and tall and graceful trees;
Here, as a various-color'd garland hung,
There, as a mantle richly-mottled flung;

Here, emulating sun-tints, lightly lie,
There, of the hues of flame spread 'neath the sky;
Here, as a gorgeous veil, the wild vines spread
And round the rugged rock their tendrils lead,
There hang umbrageous o'er the rolling flood,
Or with their crimson glories crown the wood,
And, waving to the moaning of the blast,
Responsive sigh a requiem to the past,
Their color changing with each coming morn,
Till, dark and sere, at length the rising dawn
Sees all their glory swept before the breeze
And strew'd around the bare and silent trees.
Those graceful leaves, so lightly quivering,
Kiss'd by the breath of zephyr wandering
When rose-tints on the west their blushes leave
In the soft twilight of the summer eve,
And Love upon the air comes floating by
From his bright mansion in the starry sky,
No more as harp-strings vibrate with sweet sound
And breathe melodious to the air around
Mysterious songs to charm the list'ning ear
That loves in nature's works her lore to hear,
But swept by ev'ry gale that rushes by
With eddying whirl, rudely scatter'd lie.
Then, as with musing step and list'ning ear
We tread the woodland paths, so lone and drear,
And hear the rust'ling sound still borne along,
And the sweet, mellow note of wood-bird song,
And little brook that, singing on its way,
Dances and eddies in its sparkling play,
Now, laughing, flashes back the sun's bright beam,
Now 'neath the copsewood steals with silv'ry gleam,

Now gently flows along the open mead
Where broad the fitful clouds their shadows spread,
Then in a broken cat'ract foams along,
Or glides in narrow'd channel swift and strong,
But ever with a sweet and soothing sound,
That seems the enchantment of the place around,
And with a pensiveness the spirit moves
To ope the sealed fount of all its loves.
Soft contemplation steals upon the mind,
And, to its gentle influence resign'd,
With melancholy touch'd, we love to trace
The shadow'd memories of our earthly race :
Again recall the scenes of early years
And dew them with affection's gushing tears,
While the quick promptings of the awaken'd heart
For the estrang'd fresh feeling doth impart,
And the communing soul then oft assays
The sad soliloquy of other days ;
But now imbued with firm sustaining thought
That each succeeding year the future taught,
And o'er the gloom of life the brightness throws
That cheerful hope and confidence bestows.
Oft do the feelings then apostrophize
The scenes of life as vividly they rise,
And oft in many a sorrowing word
Thus speaks the heart when deep by mem'ry stirr'd.
   Tell me what name shall I on thee bestow,
Thou source of many a joy and many a woe !
I call thee friend—we're link'd by tender ties—
And all thy faithless vows before me rise.
I call thee foe, the name my heart disclaims,
Affection's glow its fervor soon regains ;

2*

And mem'ry brings the scenes of other days,
When the warm sunshine of love's lambent rays
Play'd round our hearts, and hand in hand we stray'd
By murmuring stream beneath the beechen shade,
Or pluck'd the modest wild-flow'r from its stem,
All lovely where it bloom'd in lonely glen,
Giving its perfume to the ambient air
That in its circuit breath'd on naught more fair
Than thou wast then, a gay and laughing child,
Bounding with agile step, where ibex wild
Would scarcely venture, such the dizzy steep
That overhung the rocky, foaming deep.

Yes, memory recalls these childhood scenes
And the fair promise of maturer dreams,
And round the heart still weaves the tender chain,
That, broken, oft unites its links again.

Thus sorrowing friendship mourns its sever'd ties
As on the soul life's sweetest mem'ries rise ;
Thus in the pensive hour it loves to trace
The lines too deep for time to e'er efface,
And hoards its grief, a relic of the past,
Treasur'd with jealous care whilst life shall last ;
For, oh ! the future yields not to the soul,
Sway'd by the influences that life control,
A cup of such o'erflowing, perfect bliss,
As with its nectar dews the heart from this,
When young affections first expanded glow
On others longs its ardors to bestow,
Finds in the sympathies of some dear friend
Harmonious ties that their beings blend.

Ambitious lures may spread their gilded bait,
And pomp and fame may in attendance wait,

And sycophants may fawn with honeyed smile,
Each aimed shaft avert with ready wile,
And homage yield of honor and of praise
Till they the mortal seem to Godhead raise ;
But, ah ! the full responses of the soul
Give not their voice at vanity's control.

   And though mild virtue, with its steady ray,
Illume the rising and the setting day,
Though charity each coming hour may bless,
And future love with blandishment caress,
That memory a dark'ning shadow lies
Upon the brightness of the summer skies ;
For who the wreck of perfect faith that knows
The full meed of trust again bestows ?
And yet, oh, love ! who thee would here forego
Shall drink a deep, less mingled cup of woe.
Thou art the soother sweet of ev'ry ill,
Thou calm'st life's storms, and whisperest, Be still !
Thou alien to the earth and native of the skies,
Descends from thence, that we there may rise.
Pure and o'erflowing, ample in thyself,
Thou ask'st not worldly pomp nor worldly pelf ;
Gives without measure, of the same receives,
Nor asketh wherefore, but in love believes ;
Spreads out a boundless feast on barren ground,
And concentrates bright beams from darkness round ;
On thorny paths a soothing balsam strews,
And shakes from flow'rs of heav'n ambrosial dews ;
Exalts and purifies with holy aim,
And sanctifies from ev'ry dark'ning stain ;
With gentle hand leads in the upward road,
Till safe we reach the heavenly abode,

Where, still exalting, thou art still our guide;
In heav'n, through thee, yet more we're sanctified.
   Such art thou, love, thou heav'n-descended guest;
Such art thou here, thou blessing of the blest!
   The mother watching o'er her infant child,
Low singing ditties in the woodland wild,
Feels through her breast thy holy influence spread:
Visions of bliss are hov'ring o'er her head.
What pure aspiring through her bosom burns,
As to that form of innocence she turns!
The checker'd past she weeps with mingled tears,
And love maternal wakes a thousand fears.
Thick lie the ills of life, its joys are snares,
And evil lurks in pleasures and in cares:
A holier energy her bosom fires,
A holier aim a fresh resolve inspires
To wrestle yet for gifts of heav'nly grace,
Upon that infant soul pure lines to trace.
   Years roll away; the aim that then awoke
The binding fetters from her spirit broke.
With purpose lofty and with effort high,
She seeks an heritage above the sky,
That she may lead him to the blest abode,
To join the angel-worship there of God.
   Sweet infancy! where'er thy voice is heard
How from its depth the fount of feeling's stirr'd!
Thy helplessness, thy young and budding grace,
Express'd in lineament of form and face;
The aid of love implor'd with many a tear,
Repaid by smiles and murmurs soft and clear;
The sweet endearment of thy glad caress,
Thy gushing joy, that sadness oft may bless,

And win the thoughts from brooding sorrow's smart
To cheerful hope and peacefulness of heart.
These, helpless infancy, are thine to give;
These, young immortal, in thy being live.
Blest state, that stirs within the deepest deeps,
And fresh the fount of human feeling keeps!
  But, ah! who looks on thee, by all caress'd,
With blandishment of word and action bless'd,
Nor for thy future heaves an anxious sigh,
And fears for griefs that now may hover nigh?
Before thee lies the ever-open road,
That lures the footsteps from the path of good;
Malignant passions wait on thee to prey,
And guilt to stain the pureness of thy day,
Whilst harsh unkindness many a thorn may strew,
Or pierce with venom'd shaft thy bosom through,
Embittering the opening dawn of life
With sorrow, through a long existence rife,
Whilst they who loved and would have been thy shield,
Inert in death, to thee no care may yield.
  But Nature kindly in thy bosom pours
Joy from her pure and still exhaustless stores;
To thee she gives, at close of summer day,
When slow the sun descends, with lengthen'd ray,
To wander where the gently-rippled wave
The beds of coral and of sea-shells lave,
And gather treasures from the briny deep,
The while, unknown to thee, thy feelings steep
Themselves in influence that future time
May ripen for the harvest of heaven's clime;
And when the genial spring her buds unfold,
And rich the promise shows in green and gold,

When the blithe blackbird comes with crimson'd wing,
And on the leafless boughs the robins sing,
How then the spirits in the young heart dance!
What wealth of joy they see in time's advance!
What vernal treasures show in ev'ry nook,
Where the south wind his balmy wing has shook!
The wealth of childhood are those springing flow'rs,
The notes of songsters and the shade of bowers,
That memory through future time shall keep,
When the blanch'd brow with care is furrow'd deep,
And oft shall pause, with retrospective sigh,
At eventide, beneath the calm, clear sky,
To think how few of all the joys here known
Thrill through the heart as those with childhood flown.
    Yet, as we trace life's ever-devious road,
Expectance cheers with hope of promis'd good;
Rich sun-tint o'er the uncertain future spreads,
And paints in life's dull wastes enamel'd meads; .
The youthful heart buoys with fair dreams of bliss,
And gives the nectar of heaven's life to this.
What sweet illusions trance the ardent mind!
Fancy exalts, affections pure, refined,
Sees in the vista of the coming years
A thornless path undew'd with sorrow's tears,
A happy home where cares can ne'er annoy,
And where undying love sheds light and joy.
    Ah! think thou not, fond mortal, to possess
More than an equal share of happiness;
For know it is decreed to all below
One common lot to share of joy and woe;
Though thou awhile may proudly pass along,
And deem beneath thy care the humble throng,

With them thou shar'st the joys and ills of life,
The heart's warm rapture, and the passions' strife,
The ardent wish, the disappointed aim,
The expectation sweet that fed the flame
Of fancy's visions bright, ere they to manhood
    came.
    That home of promis'd joy to thee may be
The witness of thy heart's deep misery.
The best some kind indulgence still must claim,
Forbearance be an oft-remembered name,
And e'en forgetfulness true love must know,
If its pure, welling spring shall freely flow;
Or carelessness aside may turn the stream,
Or seeming coldness check its sunny gleam.
Distrust full oft the boded evil brings,
Estrangement from its baneful influence springs,
And hearts where warm affections inly burn
Indifference with indifference return,
Repress of kindly words and deeds the flow,
Till angry passions scathing glow,
Uncheck'd by the pure love given
From the source of love in heaven.
    How blest are they who through existence prove
Life's gentle blandishments in wedded love!
To smooth the roughness of the daily road,
And lend a grace to common ill and good,
To scatter flowers where thorns thickly lie,
And blunt the dart of sorrow's hov'ring nigh;
Nor carelessness nor selfishness impart
The frequent wounds that grieve a feeling heart,
Nor with exacting spirit still require
Needless observances unjust, that tire,

But gentle virtues with the sterner blend,
And each a grace unto the other lend ;
For these, apart, imperfect leave the whole,
And contradictions strange perplex the soul.
　　O'erwrought expectances full oft create
The direst evils of our earthly state.
The mind, embittered by the poignant dart
That disappointment sends into the heart,
Turns from the fount whence the sweet waters flow,
And drugs the cup of life with needless woe ;
Sows only tares where flowers might blossom still,
Then curses Fate for ev'ry self-wrought ill.
　　Oh, woman ! should thy lot with such be cast,
Where wilt thou hide thee from the blighting blast ?
Man, sterner man, may fly his loveless home,
Bus'ness may draw, for pleasure he may roam,
The courtesies of friends, unchid, may share,
And half forget awhile his heart's despair ;
But thou? Ah, whither? No other home hast thou,
And meekly must thou bear, with placid brow,
Hide in thy bosom's core the fest'ring wound,
And fear but with thy life thy woes to bound ;
Nor sisters, nor a mother's ear, may know
The source from whence thy daily sorrows flow,
For the aspersion of a husband's name
Would tinge thy pearly cheek with hues of shame.
The high resolve to thee remains alone
To tread the path that duty still may own ;
Thy mournful happiness, to truly know
Thy purpose firm amid severest woe ;
Unwav'ring still, though each passing day
Sees fainter burn hope's slow-expiring ray,

And all thy cares and all thy labors bring
The memory of griefs thy heart that wring.
 When laid thy wreath of promise in the dust,
Despair not thou ; look up to heav'n and trust.
See'st thou yon vault where stars nightly burn
In light o'erflowing from the central urn ?
And yet beyond, where thought can never reach,
Nor Godlike science human wisdom teach ?
Profuse as gems there suns cluster'd burn
O'er worlds whose year sees centuries return,
Ere they the measure of their orbs have run,
The spring-time of their seasons but begun,
When earths, as ours, upon the dim verge hung,
Perchance to spheres remote their dirge have sung ;
Their purposes fulfill'd in that decree
That links the finite with infinity,
And gather'd back to chaos, whence they came,
Expire with time in world-consuming flame.
 Than these, more valued in thy Maker's sight
Art thou,—in thee more glorious the light.
The rays created from those orbs that shine
Reveal to that which in thee is divine
Material forms ; they shall cease to be :
The spark in thee shall burn eternally,—
An emanation from the primal source
Omnipotent ; it guides thee in thy course ;
It leads thy spirit back from whence it came,
A pure, inspiring, vivifying flame,—
A bright light shining on thy path, 'tis giv'n
To point the painful way from earth to heav'n ;
And all the sorrow here thy spirit knows,
And all the joy benignant Heav'n bestows,

3

A moral discipline to thee may be
To make thee worthy of eternity.
Death, kindly death, shall ope to thee the door
Of that blest state where thou shalt grieve no more.
There shalt thou tune thy lyre, there join the praise
That the redeem'd for their salvation raise ;
Increasing joy through endless ages prove,
Throughout them taught, how great the debt of love ;
There trust the chosen of thy heart may be
Amid the bowers of immortality.
Won by thy love, by thy unceasing pray'r,
By the endearments of thy tender care,
The root of bitterness away be cast,
And fruits of happiness mature at last.
There gather fruits of that bless'd tree of heav'n,
Whose leaves are for the nation's healing giv'n ;
Drink of the crystal stream that freely flows
From out the throne of God, and life bestows ;
Dwell in the glow of celestial light,
Such as can only bear an angel's sight ;
The light of God to that pure city giv'n,
Where live in bliss the souls redeemed to heav'n ;
Where kings their glory and their honor bring,
Where night no more shall spread its shrouding wing,
Nor grief nor sickness dim with tears the eyes
Of those made pure by Christ's great sacrifice.
God and the Lamb's pervading spirit there
The temple is, and walls proportion'd fair
Shut out what'er beatitude can pain,
Or on its brightness cast a dark'ning stain ;
Along its golden streets to measures move
Of lyres forever tuned to joy and love.

And yet, perchance, with mournful song their strings
May sometimes vibrate as memory brings
Visions that flit, as dim remember'd dreams,
With a sweet sadness, of terrestrial scenes,
As the entranced soul looks back to trace
From the resplendence of its resting-place
The griefs and sorrows of life's pilgrimage,
As oft with fainting step it walk'd earth's stage,
And falter'd oft along the devious way,
As with uncertain light it sought truth's ray;
Its clear perception dimm'd by craving sense,
That importuned, with purposes intense,
To lure it from the self-denying road
And seek to fill its wants with earthly good,
To check its aspirations to arise
And claim its heritage above the skies;
To chain the eternal attributes of mind
To forms as fleeting as the passing wind.
Then higher bid the song of praise to flow,
Then purer feel the flame of love to glow,
For grace imparted from those thralls to free,
And seek the treasures of eternity.
Cast down your golden crowns before the throne
And join the symphony to Thee alone,
For Thou all things created by Thy pow'r,
And we through Thee share this triumphant hour !
    He there with Thee through endless ages know
Of love and knowledge the increasing flow,
Through the immensity of space profound
See orbs with glow resplendent circle round,
Not dim, remote, as in the far obscure,
But in the full effulgence of their sphere,

And hear the choral song of joy they breathe
As they their mystic dance harmonious weave,
And with the spirit's heav'n-illumin'd eye
Search of the works of God the mystery.

What passes in the heart no tongue can tell,
No human eye can see what there does dwell;
There keen remorse and sorrow, grief and pain,
Whilst in the face do peace and pleasure reign;
Dire malice there may nurse her reptile brood
And through each day concoct her bitter food,
And stern revenge may lurk beneath the smile
That lures its victim with its venom'd guile,
And passion there may roll its headlong tide,
Sapping each virtue in its passage wide,
Unseen, unknown, to any eye below,
Until each vice has wrought its work of woe;
Yet still beneath, though hid from mortal eyes,
The spark of Godhead unextinguish'd lies.

As the volcano in its fitful ire
Pours forth impetuous the lava fire,
Spreading destruction in its heedless path,
Wing'd with a demon's speed, a demon's wrath,
Till o'er the peopled and the fruitful plain
Grim solitude with ruin holds its reign;
Barren as adamant, the waste around
Spreads desolate above the teeming ground;
Nor fruit nor flow'r a grateful influence shed,
Nor spreading tree lifts up its shading head;
Accurs'd of God and man it seems to lie,
Nor yields of seed to earth nor incense to the sky.

Soft blows the air, the dews of heav'n descend,
And sun and rain their genial influence blend,
The bleak, black waste to fost'ring soil is turn'd,
And fruitful fields appear where lava burn'd.
Then waft the winds of heav'n the various seed,
And spread promiscuous; then of the husband need,
Lest noxious weeds insidious extend,
And from the soil the precious sepals rend;
But, these with fost'ring care taught to arise,
Wide wave the harvests 'neath the smiling skies,
And lofty trees their grateful coolness lend
And shade and shelter with their grandeur blend,
And when loud roars around the gusty blast,
Threat'ning a storm destructive as the past,
Deep soul-ton'd voices answer to the wrath,
Harmless the tempest speeds upon the path.
Harmonious sounds are softly breath'd around,
And all is hush'd as though 'twere holy ground,
While 'neath their shadow the meek flow'rets lie
With modest grace and heav'n-turning eye.
So, when the human heart assoiled by sin
Has felt the burning ravages within,
A desolation bleak and bare and dread
Its blackness o'er the blasted soul has spread,
Hopeless of good, a ruin'd wreck it lies,
Nor upward dares to turn its darken'd eyes.
Should then some spirit wake the latent fire,
Till heav'nward the smould'ring flames aspire,
And on the wings of aspiration borne
It hail the rising of a moral morn;
Yet, where of clinging guilt is many a cloud
That hangs on the horizon as a shroud,

Dark'ning the clearness of the mental day
As o'er its face the changing passions play,
Yet, as with lofty aim and steady eye
The enkindled soul maintains its purpose high,
Bright rise the flames, the clouds disperse in air,
And heav'n outspreads, with aspect clear and fair,
Where many a galaxy of mellow'd beam
Sheds forth of fost'ring light a living stream,
That germinate the seeds of heav'n on earth,
And many a latent virtue calls to birth,
Till fruits immortal, worthy of the skies,
From out the seeming wreck and ruin rise.
Alas! how often the awaken'd spirit
In vain seeks for the good it would inherit!
No soothing voice sustains it in its course,
No gentle hand pours balm when wounds remorse.
The still, small voice within, to him unknown,
Repress'd, unheeded, from his breast has flown,
Or, hid beneath the growing guilt of years,
Is sought in vain with sighs and burning tears.
He knows not whither in his guilt to fly,
On him Heav'n frowns with an avenging eye;
The penal fires are bursting 'neath his tread,
And fearful darkness gathers round his head;
Remorse, despair, hold empire o'er his soul,
And judgment's awful thunders o'er him roll;
In the engulfing stream of crime he lies,
And fear shuts out hope's promise from his eyes.
Ah, then, had Heav'n in its goodness lent
Some sympathizing friend, in mercy sent
To pour the balm in his contrited heart,
And holy aid and counsel to impart,

To point him to the monitor within,
That disenthrals the tangled web of sin,
And sheds heav'n's clearness on the fearful path,
Where dark and lurid gleam the clouds of wrath!
But, left with fear alone, upon his way
No lambent star shines with benignant ray,
But meteor-gleams delusive meet his sight,
That pass, and darker glooms the shrouding night.
    Blest sympathy, thou soother sweet of life,
More light thou mak'st the ills with which 'tis rife;
Blest are the links of thy uniting chain,
That thrills the heart with others' joy and pain,
Widens the sphere of human love and bliss,
And brings the joys of other worlds to this.
Through thee shall carking care flee far away,
That brings with sorrow premature decay;
The stricken one no more, with weary tread,
Shall hover round the scenes of pleasure fled,
Nor lonely pine o'er the deserted hearth,
With tearful eyes, rememb'ring scenes of mirth
That gladdened once their pilgrimage on earth.
    Thine is the pow'r, O Sympathy! to shed
A calming unction, as oil on water spread
Round the toss'd bark, when the tempestuous ocean,
Heaving and sinking, in the wild commotion
Threatens to bury, in engulfing graves,
Whatever meets its fearful, storm-toss'd waves;
But gently, gently, does its force subside,
Calm, as o'er summer seas the vessels glide,
When the soft fluid shields their troubled breast
From adverse winds that vex'd their tranquil rest.

Whate'er the lot on earth that we may claim,
How high upon the roll prefer our name,
Or in the humble walks with care to tread,
And feel life's various ills around us spread,
Enough remains to each of pain and sorrow
To dim the present and the coming morrow,
To draw to all of sympathy the flow,
For all are link'd in brotherhood of woe.

Oh, wouldst thou know the value of this life,
Its joy, its care, its sorrow, and its strife,
Hang with suspended feeling o'er the forms,
And watch the spirit, parting in the storms
Of elements conflicting, as decay
O'er them asserts its fast dissolving sway;
Mark the departing breath, as yet more faint
Is heard the moaning and expiring plaint;
That face, so lovely in the bloom of health,
That brow, where glittered India's gorgeous wealth,
Now overspreading with death's pallid hues,
Now moist with sinking nature's clammy dews;
The limbs contorted and the clinch'd hands grasp'd,
And then relaxing as the spirit pass'd,
Until, compos'd and calm, the tranquil clay
As in sweet early childhood's slumber lay,
With no remembrance of life's changing ill,
With no more conflict of rebelling will,
As if an angel at the soul's release
On it the signet set of perfect peace,—
Of perfect peace, as the soul wings away;
But what is left to mourners of the clay?
Then thrillingly awakes the feelings' strife,　　•
And, with fond madness, would call back to life

From the eternal mansions of repose
The soul, again to combat with life's woes ;
Nor yet can realize the rending scene,
But, with the indistinctness of a dream,
In that sad moment concentrated years
Come with their memories of smiles and tears :
The varied past, the joyless future, blend,
And with their poignancy the bosom rend,
Till, all subdued the soul, and anguish riv'n,
The humbled mourner turns for hope to heav'n.
    To heav'n, of our eternity the goal,
The port of hope to ev'ry weary soul,
Whose beams divine illume the gloomy road
That to the spirit opes the blest abode.
How dark that road ! but through its vista far
Shines out with purest light a radiant star ;
On the dread pathway sends its cheering gleams,
And on the future sheds effulgent streams,
Revealing, ere the narrow gulf be pass'd,
The blest fruition of our faith at last.
O Death ! to thee we raise the grateful strain :
If not for thee, then life indeed were pain.
When presses on the soul of ill the load,
How oft thou seem'st the boon of greatest good !
How sweet beneath the grassy turf to lie,
In the soft twilight of the summer sky,
The aching heart hush'd in its last repose,
No more alternate throbs with joys nor woes !
And whether yet by joy or woe possest,
Its yearning vain for happiness unblest.
Some sad vacuity left aching there,
Some longing unassuaged by joy nor care,

Some aspiration of the eternal mind,
Which we would seek in vain on earth to find.
But thou, O Death ! the veiling mantle rends,
And full life to the soul its pow'r extends ;
The pure Elysium of its hope then gains,
And with the wasted garment leaves its pains.
　As wreaths of mist upon the mountain's height
All lovely show in morn's uncertain light,
In forms fantastic graceful change and break,
And lovely scenes to fancy's visions make,
Yet ever varying in the rosy light,
The show whose beauty doth the eye delight,
And glowing still in the reflected beams,
Its shadows brighten with the golden gleams,
While breathing harmonies the soul inspire,
With elevated thought and pure desire.
But when the mounting orb ascends on high,
And clear the light illumes the radiant sky,
Th' enchanted scenes disperse in empty air,
And rough and rugged stand the cliffs and bare,
And moaning tempests sigh a fitful blast,
Where dulcet airs refreshing lightly pass'd,
And yawning gulfs and deserts intervene,
Where golden tints fell brightest on the scene,
From which the trav'ler fain would shrink afraid,
By the rude path and wounding points dismay'd :
So falls on opening youth the inspiring glow
Of joy from Iris' many-tinted bow ;
So the melodious song her voice respires
Fans the bright flame of unattain'd desires ;
But, as the sun of life ascends on high,
The hues illusive fade before the eye ;

The increasing light the paths more doubtful show,
And shadows rest where beam'd the brightest glow;
The cheerful song is mingled oft with sighs,
And gloom portentous shrouds expectant eyes;
Devious appears the once guiding ray,
And Sorrow waits where Hope erst led the way.
Yet let not anguish seize the heart, for Time,
With rapid flight, speeds on his course sublime,
And bears to Death.   And what is it to die?
To gain the life of our eternity!
That life unknown, progressive still to know?
The heart recoils: a state of joy or woe?
In what our lives have been the answer lies,—
Still lower yet to fall, or higher rise.
" Eye hath not seen, nor can the heart conceive,
The good prepar'd for those who here believe."
This graciously the Eternal Word reveal'd,
To mortals else irrevocably seal'd.
This to the soul imparts faith's fervent glow,
And through all ills sustains the heart below;
A beacon-light upon the shrouding gloom,
That lies on what awaits beyond the tomb.
Sustain'd by this the soul with faith adores,
When adverse fate its keenest sorrow pours,
Meets life's conflicting storms with heart elate,
Nor shrinks from direst ills that here await.
He sees of life the bright and rosy hue
Fade with the freshness of the morning dew;
Marks gath'ring storms on the horizon's verge,
And hears the warning of the distant surge;
With firm resolve pursues his onward way,
Though battling storms await meridian day.

The hurtling lightning and the thunders dread
Rend heaven's vault with hurrying clouds o'erspread;
By faith sustain'd he rises in that hour
Superior in indomitable pow'r.
The warring clouds recede, and glory beams
On his descending day-increasing streams,
Till, when the horizon's verge his footsteps gain,
It lies one vast and glory-tinted plain,
From whence diverging rays are richly shed
Upon the past and to the future spread,
And calm, ascending in a glow of light
A halo, rests upon the closing night.

THE GOOD-NIGHT.

Hastes, hastes, now hastes the day
When we calm in earth shall lay;
Brightly, brightly sets the sun,
His course, his course is nearly run;
Clouds are parting in the west;
Halcyon is the hour of rest.

On the coronal of night
Beams a mild and radiant light;
From the far, far depths above
Shine out eyes of light and love.
They shall guide us to the last;
They shall gild the weary past.

The weary past, with glad delight,
Now we bid the earth good-night;
Farewell blighted hopes and joys;
Farewell all that peace destroys;
Farewell boding grief and sorrow,—
Hail now to the dawning morrow!

The dawning morrow brightens yet;
Let us all the past forget;
Boding grief and carking sorrow
Merging in that bright'ning morrow;
The future radiant with delight,—
With joy, O Earth, to thee! Good-night.

HYMN OF DEATH.

THEY are there, they are there, in that happy land
Upon the bright sea, a bless'd, gather'd band;
The amaranth crowns their pure temples wear,
And far, far from them are sorrow and care.

Their harps are all strung to anthems of praise;
Sweet are the songs they joyously raise,
Rejoicing in bliss on earth that not even
The saints ever dream'd of tasting in heaven.

My sisters, my brothers, I hasten to you,—
Cold on my brow of death lies the dew;
But my hope is more strong, my faith is more clear,
As the shadows of earth from my soul disappear.

Methinks I now hear an anthem clear ringing,
The song of redemption the angels are singing;
A sinner is rescued, his feet gain the shore,
The swellings of Jordan can reach him no more.

The gathering folds of Death's curtain are round me,
In coldness and gloom it seems to enshroud me;
But a radiance divine on my dim eye is beaming,
And music's rich tones on my cold ear are streaming.

A mortal of earth his eternity gains;
Immortal, he rises redeem'd from his stains;
In the song of the Lamb henceforward to join,
The earthly transform'd to the pure and divine.

LINES

SUGGESTED ON SEEING A YOUNG LADY LEFT BY HER NEAREST RELATIVES IN HER LAST HOURS.

OH! let not strangers' eyes upon me look,
  Nor strangers' arms enfold my sinking form,
When Death the fatal dart has o'er me shook,
  That chills the current of my life-blood warm.

But let those friends, who in life were dear,
  Bend o'er my pillow at that solemn hour,
And let me feel that soothing solace near
  Which friendship oft in suff'ring's wounds may pour.

When on this world my dying hours I close,
  When of its scenes a last farewell I take,
I would my eyes should dwell the last on those
  Who made existence dearer for their sake ;

For whom my prayers ascended morn and even,
  Wafted with earth's incense on the air,
That we, beyond yon star-extended heaven,
  Together might celestial pleasures share.

Oh ! false to nature's tend'rest, holiest feeling,
  Who, shrinking from the closing hour of anguish,
Wait not the fullness of Death's dread revealing,
  But leave his prey without their balm to languish.

While yet the vital spark sustains the flame,
  When consciousness to the mute gaze seems past,
Oft does not love intensely thrill the frame,
  Of all our mortal pangs expiring last ?

Our love of our eternity is part ;
  Not with the failing frame does it decay ;
Oft it warm fervors kindles at the heart
  As the unfetter'd spirit wings away.

Oft, as with prophetic power revealing,
  What words of rapture from its teaching flow,
As heav'nly visions to its gaze unsealing
  It tastes on earth the bliss that angels know !

'Tis then thy pow'r, oh harmony divine !
  Hovers upon the consecrated hour,
And the rapt spirit leaves its prostrate shrine,
  Confiding in a Saviour's saving pow'r.

Shall mortals, then, shrink from that holy scene,
  Nor learn the solemn lesson by it taught?
How passing vain our earthly cares have been!
  How great the joy through death unto us brought!

THE SOLDIER'S LIFE OF LOVE AND GLORY.

IN a gallant ship we cross'd the main
And march'd unto an Indian plain;
We fought beneath a scorching sun;
And thus our glorious race begun.

We heard the dreaded tiger's howl,
The fierce hyena's famish'd growl,
The crocodile lay in the brake,
And near us coil'd the venom'd snake.

We fought again, and yet again,
And farther went from the cooling main;
Fatal miasma in the air
Laid many a youthful comrade there.

By day the heat, by night the dew,
Their dire attacks on us renew;
And in the family of pain
Came hunger, with her fearful train.

Thus slowly pass'd the years away,
And our dark locks were turn'd to gray,
When we with joy heard the command
Homeward to sail and then disband.

The sails were set, the wind was fair,
And fav'ring blew the balmy air,
As we bade farewell to the fatal shore,
To hail our native land once more.

The fav'ring gale still bore us on,
In liquid light the ocean shone,
And pleasing dreams our hearts inspire
With hope and joy's forgotten fire.

The gales still blow, the sun still shines,
In gorgeous gold and red declines,
But on the horizon's farthest verge
A cloud lay dark'ning o'er the surge.

With thunder peal and lightning's flash,
The raging waters round us dash :
The ship lies buried 'neath the wave;
There all my mates have found a grave.

Upon a wave I rose at last
And seized a boat that drifted past,
While high it rose with bound and shiver,
Then seem'd to sink, ay, and forever.

I tried to pray; the heavens were dark,
The winds were howling round my bark,
The lightning's lurid' flash alone
Gleamed upon the crested foam.

Upon the wide sea's yawing wave
My bark seem'd gulf'd within its grave,
But it rose a mountain height,
As with thunder-peal broke forth the light.

No human voice upon the storm
Was heard from night till rise of morn,
But battling tempests round me hung,
And death-like dirges round me sung.

I deemed my hour was come at last,
And thought glanc'd o'er the checker'd past,
And even then my heart beat high,
As the scenes came back of infancy.

The shaded bow'r rose fair to view,
With flow'rs gay glist'ning in the dew,
And the little plot before the door,
Where my mother told old legends o'er.

Ah, there we stood, a merry band,
With tripping feet, link'd hand in hand,
And in sportive mirth and childish glee
Breathed out the joy of infancy.

How peaceful seem'd the cottage scene,
The spreading tree and verdant green !
The howling storm no more I heard,
Home and its joys alone appear'd.

But, then, the rattling clouds of heav'n
By thunder and by lightning riv'n,
Broke startling on my tranced ear,
And wild, convulsed waves appear.

Oh heav'ns! it was a fearful sight:
My soul still trembles with affright,
Though safe upon the shore I stand,
And rock-protected is the land.

The morning dawn'd and hope beat high,
The sun rose glorious in the sky;
The tempest clouds had pass'd away
And ripples o'er the waters play.

My little bark still drifted on,
My course unknown, my compass gone,
But now, oh joy! upon my sight
Far rose a coast in the morning light.

Yet fanning gales bore on my bark,
I near'd it as the night grew dark,
And with the cheerful rising morn
Fair lay to view the hill and lawn.

I sprang upon the sanded shore,
I quickly trac'd the wide beach o'er;
I stood before the cottage door,
There sang my mother as of yore.

Grandchildren sat upon her knee,
While stood around my sisters three,
And my brothers told in many a story
Of a soldier's life of love and glory.

They little knew of the temptings sore
That break the peace to return no more,
Nor the peril and grief by land and sea,
In the life they pictured so gloriously.

But when they saw my worn-out look,
They came, and each a hand they took,
And never more did they tell the story
Of a soldier's life of love and glory.

THE CONSCRIPT.

WHERE sleep'st thou now? The sunset tints are fading,
  And night is gathering o'er the azure sky,
Faint, curling mists are objects dim o'ershading,
  And winds are singing low their lullaby.

Where sleep'st thou now? The trump has ceas'd its
      sounding,
  The war-note deep is hushed the hills among,
And purple vintage-grounds are now resounding
  With festive glee breath'd forth in many a song.

When the young spring its odors sweet was lending
  To every breeze that wooingly pass'd by,
When the bright summer its green leaves was blending
  In shadow deep with sunlight of the sky,   ·

I saw thee, boy, with health upon thy brow,
  Swift as the chamois on the mountain height,
Climb the high avalanche of spotless snow
  And stand exulting in the glowing light.

Thy spirit, free as eaglet of the mountain,
　Expanded with the glory of the sight,
As thou, with voice glad as the gush of fountain,
　In ecstacy pour'd forth thy wild delight.

Conscription came; how fell thy flutt'ring pinion
　To soar no more through regions of the air!
Thou stood in marshal'd ranks of pow'r the minion,
　Thou, my free-hearted boy, my tend'rest care.

Where sleep'st thou now? When ev'ning softly closes,
　How sorrow presses with its shades on me !
And when in quiet deep the earth reposes
　My soul goes forth in gloom in search of thee.

Mid heaps of slain, my son, I see thee lying,
　Unshrouded, on a far, unhallow'd soil ;
Low, dirge-like notes the cold night wind is sighing ;
　To glory what are poverty and toil?

For them the trump of Fame wakes not its breathing,
　To future time no clarion tells their name,
For them fair hands no laurel chaplet wreathing,
　Their deeds no chosen bard shall e'er proclaim.

They stood where fiercest rag'd the shock of battle,
　They stood where loudest volleying cannon roar'd,
They stood unvalu'd as brute-driven cattle,
　As round the hissing shot, death-dealing, pour'd.

My son, thou liest on the battle-ground
　With those who, falling, ne'er are named again ;
Vain unto such of Fame the vaunted sound,
　There glory hides her heaps of buried slain.

THE SLAVE FIEND.

MURKY is the midnight air,
Lurid is the lightning's glare ;
Winds are howling through the trees,
Moaning blasts come on the breeze,
Thunder rolls along the air,
Loud the crash ! beware, beware !

Lo ! a stealthy, crouching form :
Is it the Ruler of the storm ?
No regal port the recreant wears,
No sceptred hand the recreant bears ;
Crime is written on his brow,
Deeds of crime await him now.

Gloating eyes and reeking hands,
Oaths by which no compact stands,
Curses burdening the air,
Breath polluting all that's fair,
These attendant on him wait,
A chosen band from Hades' gate.

Hark ! that shriek ! the rising flame
Answers to the Slave Fiend's name.
Men in deeds of blood expire,
Women feed the glowing fire ;
Happy they who thus can die
In lands beneath their native sky.

Now a sad, lamenting band
Is led unto the ocean strand ;
Early manhood and its prime,
Age bow'd 'neath the weight of time,
Childhood with its aspect fair,
All, fell fiend, thy victims are.

The mother's loud, bemoaning cry,
The wailing plaint of infancy,
The drooping maiden's tear-wet cheek,
The groans from manly breasts that break,
The mad'ning shriek of wild despair,
All attest thy presence there.

Along the desert's dreary way
Of them full many a corpse shall lay;
Ah! bless'd of that stricken number
Who at Meshroo's well shall slumber,
And where El Hammer's waters glide,
In death lay sleeping side by side.

The weary day and mournful night
Of bondage sheds its upas blight
No more upon the souls forlorn
From native land and kindred torn,
To pine beneath a foreign sky,
Or on the waves of ocean die.

Farewell home and leafy bow'rs,
Mimosa shade and gorgeous flow'rs,
Repose at noon and dance at night
Beneath the South's resplendent light.

These no more await us now,
To slav'ry's galling yoke we bow.

But beyond the waters wide
Unnumber'd ills our lot betide:
Tasks beneath the scorching sun,
From tardy hands with rigor won;
Toil beneath the open sky
When gelid winds are whistling by,
While broken hearts dry up the source
That gives to purpose nerve and force.

There no friendly voice shall greet us,
No eye shall brighten there to meet us;
In that land, by all forsaken,
No kindred hearts our joys shall waken;
Slav'ry's chain shall bind us fast,
And all the blest affections blast.

Ties of mother and of wife,
Tend'rest of the ties of life;
Ties of father and of son,
That strengthen as their course they run,
With cruel grasp thou dost dissever,
Blasting happiness forever.

Slave Fiend! these thy curses are,
With good forever still at war,
Debasing in thy demon fold
All that good and great we hold;
Crushing each aspiration high,
Till base and vile thy victims lie.

PRAYER OF THE SLAVE.

God! we are lowly, and our brothers, men,
   Look on us as the outcasts of the earth.
Wilt Thou not be a father to us, then?
   Ours are as theirs, souls of immortal birth.

Love, strong and deep, within our bosom lies,
   And sympathies that ask an answ'ring tone;
There sweet humanities, affection's ties,
   Vibrate with pulse as tender as their own.

What though Thou gave us, under burning skies,
   A skin as dark as night's ebon hue?
Within our breasts a fountain welling lies,
   Of feelings oft refresh'd by heav'nly dew.

Ours the hard lot of bitter scorn to bear,
   Of slav'ry's chain and nature's rites refus'd;
Grant us, great God! a gracious father's care,
   And in Thy mercy aid the long-abus'd.

We, too, are purchas'd by that holy blood,
   A Saviour, dying, shed upon the cross;
We with that Holy Spirit are endued
   That purges from the soul its secret dross.

But, oh! debas'd by hard oppression's sway,
    Our groveling souls with feeble wing aspire;
On us shines not the renovating ray
    That springs from Liberty's ennobling fire.

God! in Thy mercy touch the hearts of men,
    Guide them with wisdom in the path of right;
Let justice' equal scales prevail, and then
    Shall nations walk as brothers in thy sight.

Haste Thou the day when Ethiope shall come
    With outstretched arms to worship at Thy shrine;
Prepare the way and lead the chosen on
    Who spread the knowledge of Thy light divine.

Let the harsh tones of angry discord cease,
    From selfish views sublime the human heart;
Then shall the holy pow'r of heav'nly peace
    Its influence of purity impart.

SPIRIT OF THE WORLD.

YEARS are stealing on apace,
Man is speeding on his race;
Closely I his progress mark,
Childhood's light grows dim and dark;
Mists I cast before his eyes,
And deluding shades arise.

By my serpent-folds entwined,
Firmer, firmer do I bind;
Love is but the poet's theme,
Virtue's but a shadowy dream;
Thirst for pelf, dross of the spirit,
These from me he doth inherit.

Now the web is closely woven,
Now the gulf is widely cloven;
Aspirations cease to rise,
Earthward now are fixed the eyes;
Earth holds the spirit in my pow'r,
It becomes my rightful dow'r.

These the treasures that I bring,
As time speeds on with silent wing;
The pure dreams of early youth,
The love of virtue and of truth,
Vanish as my chains I bind
Round those by my folds entwin'd.

TO THE WIND.

OH, wind of heaven! thou dost pass
   O'er ocean wild upheaving,
O'er morass wild, o'er prairie grass,
   O'er desert, eye deceiving.

Oh, still thou breathest in thy flight
   O'er graves and pale corse mouldering,

O'er age, o'er youth, o'er childhood's light,
    Gone from life's path bewildering.

But thou bearest no note in thy many-ton'd lyre
    Of the secrets deep of death,
Though in thy wailings thou seem'st to respire
    A dirge to the parting breath.

In vain thee we ask of the charnel dark,
    Of the work that is doing there;
In vain thee we ask of the wasting bark
    That once was our dearest care.

Thou passest on and thou answerest not;
    We list to thy voice in vain,
As we cherish our memories unforgot
    In a bosom filled with pain.

Thou passest on and thou answerest not,
    And our hearts are heaving wild,
As thou wailest through the bower and grot
    Where the lost in life have smiled.

Hast thou no voice, O wandering wind,
    Of the land where they have gone?
From them no tone can'st thou leave behind
    As thy course thou speedest on?

Vainly we ask of earthly things
    The mysteries of death;
The spirit plumes its folded wings
    With the expiring breath.

The ambient air retains no trace,
   The earth no impress bears
Of the parted, whose unshrouded grace
   An angel's form now wears.

THE GOLD-DUST GATHERER.

My home! my home! my sunny home,
   Beneath the far blue skies,
Ah, wherefore from thee did I roam,
   To where cold mountains rise?

The streams adown their cliffs that flow,
   Though rich with golden ore,
To my sad heart no joys bestow;
   Why should I seek them more?

Brighter to me the sparkling eyes,
   Under the palm-tree shade,
Than gems with their unclouded dyes,
   That here their bed have made.

More sweet to me the lute-like tone
   Of the low-whisper'd voice
Of her that there I call my own,
   Than wealth's delusive joys.

Again I'll seek the palm-tree's shade,
　Upon the flow'ry plain.
Ah, woe is me that thence I strayed!
　I'll haste to it again.

TO A BIRD SINGING IN THE AIR.

Bird with quick wing upspringing,
　Caroling cheerily, cheerily,
What in the air art thou singing,
　Warbling so merrily, merrily?

Thy song is tuneful laughter,
　A note of merry glee,
Glad as the gushing water
　From icy fetters free.

From ev'ry breeze soft blowing
　Thou inhalest fresh delight;
From ev'ry sunbeam glowing
　Thy spirits grow more bright.

So exulting is thy minstrelsy,
　So joyous and so free,
One would deem each winged phantasy
　Were minister to thee.

Charm'd by thy note of gladness,
  We look upward to the skies,
Forgetful of the sadness
  That to earth had droop'd our eyes.

A sympathetic feeling
  Awakes within the breast;
Thy song joy's fount unsealing,
  Through thee we are bless'd.

Through the air so thrilling
  Comes the liquid gush;
All nature's pulse seems trilling
  With the mellifluous rush.

Now ravish'd with the melody
  Of thy exceeding gladness,
Thou hang'st pois'd in ecstasy,
  Thy notes strain'd to madness.

Then suddenly espying
  In the fresh grass thy nest,
With wing downward flying,
  Thou seek'st there thy rest.

MARGARET.

SHE dwells alone, she dwells alone,
   Upon the heath-clad hill,
Where the wind sighs in many a tone
   And leaps the gushing rill.

Day after day there rolleth by,
   And night succeeds to night;
Still wanes the pale moon in the sky,
   And stars shed down their light.

And yet no footstep on that hill,
   No voice of song is heard,
For lonely, lonely there, and still,
   No pulse her soul hath stirr'd.

She sitteth on the moss-grown stone,
   As statue mute and pale;
Around are wither'd flow'rets strown,
   Mementos of her tale.

Pluck'd from the fost'ring parent-stem,
   And scatter'd to the blast,
She casts full many a glance at them,
   And thinks upon the past.

But vague are all her thoughts and fleet,
   And vacant is her eye;
Nor is there aught that it can meet
   That prompts a smile or sigh.

Within a stately hall she grew
   To girlhood's sunny prime;
Her eye was like the sparkling dew
   In the glowing morning time,

And, as bright beams upon a flow'r,
   Smiles on her features play'd;
They pass'd, for soon the tempest's pow'r
   Her loveliness low laid.

Then fled the sweet smile from her face,
   The bright glance from her eye,
And apathy has found a place
   Where beat the young heart high.

No friendly voice responds to hers,
   No hand with gladness greets;
All's still, save when a murmur stirs,
   As a passing vision fleets.

She sitteth on a mossy stone,
   As statue mute and pale;
She sitteth there alone, alone,
   With none to list her tale.

THE VOICE AND EYES OF INFANCY.

SWEET infancy! thy tone
Hath o'er bosoms lone
  A gentle sway,
And hearts that long have slept,
And neither joy'd nor wept,
  The power obey.

Of childhood's note of glee
From inborn sympathy,
  Unspoken all by word,
But breath'd in many a sound,
Echoed in song around,
  When it the air hath stirr'd.

The warbling, soft and sweet,
Telling of visions fleet
  That flit across the mind—
The cadences that steal
When gleamings sad reveal
  The lot of human kind—

Have a prophetic tone
In many a wailing moan
  Of earthly destiny;
But the expressive eyes,
Where shadow'd the soul lies,
  Tell of eternity.

TO A CHILD.

THOUGH there is beauty on thy brow,
And thy blue eyes are sparkling now,—
Though there is bloom upon thy cheeks,
And thy tongue in accents speaks
That can charm the list'ning ear,
And sorrow's drooping victims cheer,—
Though bright the morning of thy day,
Undimm'd by clouds thy matin ray,
Careering through thy noontide sky
May storm and tempest hurtling fly,
Sorrow for thee a woof may weave
And blight upon thy life may breathe,
Ere from thy hours of joyous sport
Ambitious lures thy visions court.
For life is frail as vernal grass
That bends as zephyrs o'er it pass;
Frail as the form reflected in the lake
That the careless wand'ring wind doth break.
Uncertain still the promise of the hour,
And brooding storms unseen oft o'er it low'r,
But conscious innocence the soul can arm
Serene to meet the mightiest pow'r of harm.
Be then as the opening vestal rose,
That to the morning does its sweets disclose,
But as the day advances to the even
Drops its pure leavés, exhaling sweets to heav'n.

TO DECEPTION.

WILT thou leave me, lov'd deception?
  Wilt thou no longer round me hover,
Robed in all hues that bright conception
  In fancy's regions can discover?

Aerial as the light-wreath'd cloud,
  As ever-changing in thy hue,
Thou mantlest with delusive shroud
  Whate'er we'd gladly hide from view.

Thou dearest phantom of our youth,
  Thou architect of land of fairy,
Ere the unmasking wand of truth
  Has wav'd away our castles airy,

What shall succeed thy ruin'd pow'r?
  What visions bright shall meet our view
When thou, disfranchis'd of thy dow'r,
  For thy false beams arise the true?

Is there no charm that still can lure thee
  From youth to age on us to wait?
Is there no spell that can insure thee
  To hover round life's closing gate?

Before, with eyes unshrinking, we can bear
    The piercing brightness of truth's eagle gaze,
Before to look on life unmask'd we dare,
    Thou from thy plumage shak'st the gilded rays.

And Truth's stern form, rob'd in a sable shroud,
    In sadness on our unveil'd vision breaks,
And from thy floating cincture of bright cloud
    The rosy hue with firm endeavor takes.

Will she, in awful majesty sublime,
    Light-rob'd appear to our unfilm'd eyes,
And, triumphing above the wrecks of time,
    Sit, throned with mercy, glorious in the skies?

When, the dark portals of Death's valley pass'd,
    Hope, fear, nor gloom our varying passions sway,
But, in the certainty of bliss at last,
    Our eyes behold with light of wisdom's perfect day.

ROSES AND GARLANDS.

I PLUCK'D the wither'd roses
    That bound thy bridal brow,
I strew'd them to the wild winds,
    And where are they now?

6

I gather'd up the garlands
  That to thee their beauty gave;
I flung them careless from my hands
  Upon the ocean wave.

I would my heart's dark tablet
  No record e'er should bear
Of that which promis'd thee such bliss
  And brought to me despair.

Slow pass'd the waning year,
  And spring return'd again;
The roses bloom'd, and fair vines wreath'd
  Their garlands o'er the plain;

The song of birds rejoicing came
  Upon the balmy air,
And budding trees their op'ning bloom
  Display'd with promise fair.

But the sweet music of thy voice
  Fell not upon my ear;
I trod the woodland paths alone,
  Still list'ning to hear.

For, ah, with spring's returning reign
  Awoke my soul again,
And feeling's full and rushing tide
  Brought mingled love and pain.

I would the wither'd roses
  Again were in my clasp!
I would the faded garlands
  Again my hand could grasp!

But wind and wave have borne them
  Away, away from me;
Ah, love, what treasures had they been,
  Though faded unto thee!

A HALF-BLOWN WITHERING ROSE.

OPEN thy petals, rose!
  Look to the god of thy love;
Let not death o'er thee close
  Ere thou lookest above:
Brightly in heaven he's beaming,
Warmly his light from thence is streaming,
  Open thy petals, rose.

The queen of all flowers art thou,
  With fragrance thy bosom is fill'd;
E'en with'ring, there's grace in thee now,
  And sweets from thy clos'd leaves distill'd.

The soft summer air has blown round thee,
  Unharming the tempest has sped;
The sunbeam and night-dew have nurs'd thee,
  And heav'n protectingly spread.

In vain shall such care have been given
  And no grace be perfected in thee?
Ungrateful to earth and to heaven,
  Droops thou there witheringly?

Open thy petals, rose,
　　And inhale the full beam ;
Let not death o'er thee close
　　Till thou receive the stream
Of light and warmth in thy heart,
There to make perfect their part.
　　Open thy petals, rose !

THE LONE OLD OAK.

As some old monarch of the hill and plain,
　　In regal pride thou spread'st thy arms around,
And proudly looks upon the surging main
　　That ever greets thee with its moaning sound,

As though it mourn'd thy utter loneliness,
　　'Reft of the race that wav'd around thy prime :
Alone thou art of that old wilderness
　　That sprung free children of the soil and time.

No vassal trees bow to thy monarch form,
　　But with inherent grandeur art thou grac'd ;
Superior to each assaulting storm,
　　Thy might and majesty are undefac'd ;
So noble minds, with self-sustaining pow'r,
Unbending stand through desolation's hour.

THE INDIAN'S GRAVE.

CHAS'D as a leaf before the autumn blast,
Thy injur'd race from off the earth has pass'd,
And left thee tomb'd upon the mountain's brow,
Fit resting-place for one as free as thou :
Where in their glory the sun's rays descend,
Where starlit dews and moonlight radiance blend,
Where clouds magnificently pile on high,
And build thy monument 'twixt earth and sky;
Where the unfetter'd winds do blow around,
With a deep, solemn, wailing, dirge-like sound,
As though the spirits of the air there keep
Their vigils o'er thy everlasting sleep.
    The monuments of kings more proud may be,
And for their pomp may nations sail each sea,
But thou in dread magnificence shall lie
Beneath thy canopy of open sky,
When they are fallen to the trodden dust,
Effac'd each name, and crumbl'd ev'ry bust.

6*

TWO VOICES.

Oh, let me go to that dreamy land
  Where the sun shines down through shading trees,
Where the wave ripples o'er sparkling sand,
  And melodious tones are borne on the breeze,

Where the scent of flow'rs is wafted around
  By the breath of Zephyr, as he wanders o'er
The verdant and bright enamel'd ground,
  Where murmuring waters their freshness pour.

That dreamy land where the soul reposes
  In visions of bliss, 'mid phantoms of joy,
Our heads crown'd with poppies, our couch strew'd
    with roses,
  Let not real life our slumbers annoy.

Arouse thee ! awake ! shake from thee the fetter
  In impotent sloth thy soul's pow'rs that bind ;
Within thee behold a life richer and better ;
  Unshackle thy spirit, turn inward and find.

There lies the Arcadia that poets and sages
  Now, as a long-vanish'd loveliness, mourn ;
There lies El Dorado, that glows in the pages
  Where genius, enshrin'd, continues to burn.

A mine of rich wealth, that is ever disclosing,
   In ever-deep'ning depths of the abyss,
Treasures that lure not the soul to reposing,
   But incite to yet higher attainments of bliss.

Then arouse thee ! awake ! shake from thee the fetter
   In impotent sloth thy soul's pow'rs that bind ;
Within thee behold a life richer and better ;
   Unshackle thy spirit, turn inward and find.

ADOXA.

   ADOXA in a green bow'r lay,
Where waters rippl'd on their way ;
The violet there gave its perfume,
And the bee humm'd low its tune ;
The soft light glimmer'd in the shade,
By intermingling branches made ;
The beetle, cloth'd in sombre vest,
Paus'd awhile from toil to rest ;
The dragon-fly, with gauzy wing,
The crickets, that through summer sing,
The jetty worm, whose phosphor glow
Shines, an earthly star, below,
Gemming with light the em'rald hues
That lay beneath refreshing dews ;
And many a graceful, sylph-like form,
That seeks a covert when the storm

Threatens in the dark'ning sky,
And lightnings in the charg'd clouds lie,
There with her found safe retreat
From midnight damp and noonday heat.
　　In sweet repose the maiden lay,
Mantl'd in scarf and hood of gray;
Her dreams were lowly as the place,
For humility was her sweet grace ;
No proud aspirings fill'd her mind
And chaf'd her temper meek and kind ;
Content, she dwelt 'mong simple flow'rs
And insect tribes, and used her pow'rs,
Heav'n-giv'n, with diligence to trace
The wonders of that humble place.
And as o'er them, with thought intense, she por'd,
Her soul with beauty and with love she stor'd,
And learn'd to gently think of ev'ry thing
That crawl'd below or wav'd in air the wing ;
Nor spurn the meanest reptile of the earth,
That from Omniscient pow'r deriv'd its birth.
　　Goodness was hers, and her narrow way
Was where the footpaths through the valley lay;
And though afar the mountain's lofty height
Sparkled in morning and in noonday light,
And, at the evening's gold and purple close,
In rich magnificence before her rose,
She envied not its glory of array,
But turn'd to where the shadow'd landscape lay,
Content to dwell aloof from pride of place,
The benefactress of earth's varied race.
Where cottages are scatter'd o'er the green,
And humble life gives int'rest to the scene,

Where lowly virtue sends to heav'n its pray'r,
A gracious Father's smile of love to share,
And, through the toil and labor of the day,
Yet ofteɳ pauses with some sweet assay
Of charity, a burden'd heart to bless,
And make, through love, its load of mis'ry less;
Where long endurance to the patient mind
Brings the high virtue of a soul resign'd
To adverse fate, and, struggling yet to bear,
Yields, in its penury, a blessing care
To those more weak.   Oh, ye, who proudly claim
Honor and feeling for the titled name,
And think that unto them alone belong
The sympathies that wake the breath of song,
Go where the mother o'er her infant child*
Watcheth when the keen blast howleth wild;
When through each crevice comes the piercing wind,
And drifting snows her weary eyes oft blind;
When direst pains dart through her wasted form,
Unshielded from the coldness of the storm,
And see her, ever patient, ply her task,
A pittance small to gain from those who ask
No knowledge of the pinching want and need
Of the neglected poor their crumbs would feed;
And blesses Heav'n, in many a fervent pray'r,
For all its mercy, all its gracious care,
If to her toil-spent hours it daily give
The humblest means of sustenance to live.

---

* Suggested by a poor woman in the last stage of consumption earnestly seeking and doing work to provide clothing for her little children before her decease.

And when low wanes to her the sun of life,
Extinguish'd by the long-enduring strife
Of o'erwrought energies and wasting care,
Still fondly doth she labor to prepare
A little boon, her helpless charge to bless,
And make its sum of suff'ring something less,
Though in the effort she draw her parting breath,
And sink, o'erwearied, in the arms of death.
    The hero, marching with his armed bands,
With desolating step, through smiling lands,
Scatt'ring destruction in his ravage wide,
Staining with purple life the limpid tide,
Swells with the deeds of crime the loud acclaim,
And wakes the breath of never-dying fame.
But he who bravely bears the ills of life,
Through each progressive stage maintaining strife
With strong temptation and the fiery darts
That adverse fortune to his lot imparts,
Rising in moral grandeur as the ray
Of joy grows dim, and upon his day
The clouds of sorrow settle darker still,
Each morn foreboding yet increasing ill;
In low obscurity his path to tread,
Without the world's approving smile to shed
A halo round his steps, and to his heart
The balm of sweetest sympathy impart,
Hears no loud clarion to the world proclaim
The heroic virtues that adorn his name;
But lone, neglected, and forgotten quite,
Pursues unfalt'ringly the path of right,
Sustain'd alone by that small voice within
That purifies the soul from secret sin,

And elevates its views above the dust,
In holy hope and confidence and trust,
Till, as the bird that soars above the clouds
That from his gaze the empyrean shrouds,
He wings his broad flight in the eye of day,
And basks and revels in the golden ray,
Bathes in the floods of light that round him pour,
Impetuous hastes still higher yet to soar
Above the storms his native cliffs that hide,
And reach the fount of the o'erflowing tide,
Impell'd by ev'ry blast that keenly blows,
And o'er the earth its mantling darkness throws.

THE RETURN.

'TWAS here thou came in summer's flow'ry pride,
  With healthful brow and spirit light and gay,
For I had won thee for my happy bride,
  And years of promis'd bliss before us lay.

Where nature in her primal beauty smil'd,
  And virgin earth ungarner'd pour'd her stores,
We built our cabin in the untrodden wild,
  Beside the rushing river's sylvan shores.

Here was our Eden; we the only two
  In the vast solitude the silence broke,
Save winds that whisp'ring stole the covert through,
  As though, transfus'd, our spirits in them spoke.

All things seem'd holy that we look'd upon,
   And heav'n benignant on our labors smil'd ;
With orisons of joy we hail'd the sun,
   And tender cares our daily toil beguil'd.

A happy life ! but, as wan'd the year,
   Rose noxious vapors on the poison'd air,
And, with the wither'd leaf and ripen'd ear,
   Disease insidious spread its venom there.

Thou, bright and beautiful, wast stricken down,
   As a fair vine from the supporting tree,
Of which the blossoms were the graceful crown,
   Despoil'd and scath'd forever thence to be.

Month after month, beside thy couch of pain,
   With mournful heart my faithful watch I kept ;
With cheerful smiles still sought thee to sustain,
   And silent pray'd whene'er thou peaceful slept.

But when the spring with all its flow'rs awoke,
   And glad birds sang on ev'ry budding tree,
Thou meekly bow'd beneath the fatal stroke,
   And dark and lonely left the world to me.

With grief I laid thee in thy narrow bed,
   When stars were shining in the quiet sky,
And pray'rs were breath'd and burning tears were shed
   Upon the spot of earth where thou dost lie.

Awhile I linger'd, that I there might see
   The modest wild-flow'rs grow upon that mound,
For, ah ! methought a solace it would be
   To know their bloom and fragrance shed thee round.

For thou didst prize them in thy maiden days,
   When forth we wander'd in our early love,
And sought a shelter from the summer rays
   In cooling grot or shade of verdant grove.

And then a simple wreath thou us'd to twine
   To deck the beauty of thy wavy hair;
The snowy bloom and tendril-clasping vine
   Than pearls and emeralds in it shone more fair.

And yet I linger'd, and then bade farewell
   When the touch'd leaf hung flow'r-like on the bough,
And song of parting bird, with richer swell,
   Floated as melody from heav'n below.

I wander'd long among the haunts of men,
   A voiceless solitude their homes to me;
To mine a spirit answers in this glen:
   Home of my heart! my soul grows calm in thee.

ON HEARING A BELL TOLL.

EACH day the bell is ringing
   The knell of some departing soul;
We hear not then the angels singing,
   As through the clouds the chariots roll.

7

In sorrow and in darkness kneeling,
    We circle round the bed of death;
Light from above is not unsealing
    The mysteries of faith.

Dark and more dark the cloud is pressing
    Upon the tear-fill'd eyes;
Deeper and deeper sighs are heaving
    The heart, where sorrow lies.

Soul! that thou unto another soul might speak,
    Freed from its house of clay;
That thou the enshrouding gloom might break,
    And trace its heav'nward way!

Then grief and sighs might cease to be
    Round the sepulchral bed,
And songs of joy rise clear and free
    Where bitter tears are shed.

THE BROOK.

Oh, thou gurgling, gushing stream,
Reflecting many a sunny beam,
Brightly flowing on thy way
Through the long, long summer day,
With thee I'd joy to seek that shore
From which thou wilt return no more,

But as thou art exhal'd on high
To fall in rain-drops from the sky.
If with thee the gift were given
To mount unto the gates of heav'n,
No more to come unto this sphere
But as mercy's messenger,
How gladly would I seek the cave
Thou lavest with thy crystal wave,
And lay me in its quiet bed,
With pearly shells and pebbles spread !
Then come unseen, an angel pure,
To guide through life the footsteps sure
Of those with whom I've stray'd along
And listen'd to the warbled song
Of many a bird in covert dark,
Where the glow-worm lights his spark
Upon the bank, amid the shade
By the o'erarching branches made
Of trees that, towering on high,
Tell of centuries pass'd by.
    So sings an idler, child of earth,
And longs for the effulgent birth
Of a celestial dawn that brings
A day that has no shadowings.
But thou, O God ! a light hast giv'n,
Redeeming souls from earth to heav'n,
Still cheering on the lengthen'd way
With many a scintillating ray,
Disclosing duty as the road
That leads to happiness and God.

HER HEART GREW FAINT.

SHE wandered over hill and dale,
Then rested in a flow'ry vale,
And listen'd to Love's tender tale.
　　Her heart grew strong.

He sail'd upon the surging main,
But never more came he again :
The billow'd waters had him ta'en.
　　Her heart grew faint.

She lieth in the church-yard low,
Where piercing winter winds do blow,
And where lie long the frost and snow.
　　No more her heart grows faint.

———————

VICISSITUDES.

HAST thou not been where wild winds freshly blowing
　　Brought od'rous gladness on each passing gale ?
Hast thou not been where streamlets purely flowing
　　In each soft murmur told a gentle tale,

As the bright flashing of their gushing water,
   Glad as the tones of merriment and glee
That joyous burst from children in their laughter,
   Swift rushes onward to the boundless sea?

Hast thou not been where the enamel'd mead
   Its beauty gave to the enraptur'd sense,
And the crush'd flower from the elastic tread
   Yielded its life in breath of sweets intense?

Hast thou not been, in spring-time's early hours,
   Where the lone bird its short, sweet carol gave
To the young, bursting leaves and budding flow'rs
   Beside some wildly-rushing mountain wave?

Not such the lay it sings in summer hours,
   When love beats high within its little breast,
And its exulting song it joyous pours
   Where thick, embow'ring leaves conceal its nest.

Hast thou not mark'd when autumn's gorgeous glory
   Fled in the rushing of the hurrying blast,
The deep'ning pathos of the moral story
   Sigh'd in each wailing as it onward pass'd?

Hast thou not heard the ancient forest, bending
   To the far-sweeping of the mighty wind,
Send forth a solemn sound as though responding
   To a deep voice that secret pow'rs unbind?

Hast thou not stood where ocean madly raging
   Roll'd forward as with overmast'ring shock,
Till hush'd the storm, the chaf'd surge assuaging,
   It gently lav'd the firm opposing rock?

Hast thou not glean'd a lesson to thy reason
    From winter's fost'ring pow'r and spring's awak'ning
        reign,
Summer's short fervor, autumn's maturing season,
    And learn'd vicissitudes are not in vain ;

But from the varied page outspread before thee,
    Garner'd of wisdom for thy fleeting days,
Whether the sunshine or the storm be o'er thee,
    Forward to look, with hope and trust and praise ?

THE AWAKENED.

SUGGESTED BY A PORTRAIT OF A LADY HOLDING AN
OPEN LETTER.

THEN let me forget thee,—I'll cherish no more
    Thy mem'ry once so dear to this heart,
And all thy memorials of love I restore,
    For false and unworthy thou art.

Take back all the words thou hast breath'd in my ear,
    Take back the fond glance of thy love-lighted eye,
No longer my heart throb with hope nor with fear,
    No longer my breast heave affection's warm sigh.

Yet think not, thou false one, that dark and forlorn
    The path of the future to me shall still be,
Though the bright visions of life's early morn
    Have been dimm'd and been darkened by thee.

My soul shall arise exalted and pure,
  Unstained by thy falsehood, unharm'd by thy art,
And virtue triumphant with me shall endure,
  And heal all the anguish of this wounded heart.

FAME.

HEAREST thou not what Fame is sounding
  Among the haunts of men?
Hearest thou not whose name's resounding
  From mountain and from glen?
    I hear it not: my ear is cold,
    My eyes are dim, and I am old.

The deeds that thou hast done they're singing,
With songs of thine the air is ringing;
Thou art the theme, thine is the praise
That high to thee they joyous raise.

Alas for me! in manhood's pride
  I vainly sought that praise to gain,
And there was one then by my side
  To whom that praise had not been vain;
    But she in the cold earth sleeps,
    And there my heart its vigil keeps.

The palsied ear no clarion hears,
The bleeding heart no clarion cheers;
The balm of peace alone it seeks,
It listeth not of what Fame speaks.

ELLEN'S DREAM.

I DREAM'D a happy dream of thee ;
  Fond words thou breath'd into my ear,—
Such as thou oft did speak to me
  When I to thee was dear.

Again we sat beside the stream,
  Where murmuringly the waters glide,
And mark'd the flashing of the beam
  That sparkled in the flowing tide.

Above our heads upon the bush
  The birds sang forth their lays of love ;
Blithe notes of wood-bird and of thrush
  Blended with cooing of the dove.

One little hour I liv'd again,—
  . Such life as I with thee did live
When my young heart untouch'd with pain,
  Thou gav'st me all was thine to give.

Ah, woe is me, and woe the day
  When dark distrust between us came
And took the light of love away,
  But left with each a with'ring flame !

HEPATICA TRILOBA.

FROM the thin soil of mossy-crevic'd rock,
  In woodlands lone, thy roots untended spring,
Where the rude tempest's elemental shock
  Scatters destruction from his wrathful wing.

All unresisting through the stormy hours,
  Meekly thou clingest to thy parent bed,
Maturing in thy heart fair, clust'ring flow'rs,
  Whose gentle beauty round the spot will shed,

When the gay spring asserts her early sway,
  Charms that call forth a thrill of pure delight,
Luring fair nature's worshipers away
  From gauds that dazzle but ne'er glad the sight,
To muse where cavern'd waters' babbling gush
Breaks the deep stillness of the lone glen's hush.

THE GREENWOOD TREE.

COME with me to the greenwood tree
  When the sun is bright and high,
And, sitting there, view nature fair,
  And the clouds float through the sky.

The birds sing sweet, as now is mete,
　　Upon a summer day ;
The gurgling stream reflects the beam
　　Of a golden ray.

The flow'rets fair are blooming there
　　'Gain in Eden's freshness ;
Though the serpent feeds 'mong the weeds,
　　Of him we are reckless.

The greenwood tree is befitting me
　　When summer suns are shining ;
While sitting there I have no care,
　　My heart knows no repining.

――――――

GRAVE OF A MANIAC BY THE SEA.

THOU laid down to rest
　　Beside the sea surge,
And from ocean's breast
　　Arose the wild dirge.

Thou laid down to rest
　　When the tempest was high,
And the billowy crest
　　Rose white to the sky.

The sea-bird was flitting
　Through the dark, troubled air;
A wild song, befitting
　For requiem, was there.

Thou lone and sad stranger,
　From whence didst thou come?
Thou worn, houseless ranger,
　Thou now hast a home.

Nature's devotion
　Shall mantle thy grave,
Spray of the ocean
　The long grass shall lave.

The sunbeam, that long ne'er
　Thy sad heart did lighten,
Shall often that spot cheer
　And its loneliness brighten.

When death came to thee
　How wild was thy eye!
Now calmly rest thee
　Beneath the wide sky.

The storm-cloud no more
　Shall awaken thy sleep,
Thy griefs to deplore
　And sad vigils to keep.

The peace of the grave
　As a mantle enfolds thee;
Life's wildering wave
　No more shall inclose thee.

In peace art thou not
  'Mid the sea's restless motion ?
Peace, peace is thy lot
  When storms vex the ocean.

MOTHER'S LOVE.

I LOOK on thee, my lovely child,
  Upon thy gentleness and youth,
Thy spirit, ever sweet and mild,
  Thy soul aspiring after truth.

Thou, as the morning star, to me
  Broke on the night of my despair ;
I look'd upon thy radiant eye,
  And saw the pure light shining there.

And sorrow took a soften'd hue
  When that glad look was on me beaming ;
Again I saw the good and true
  That erst appear'd a fabled seeming.

For those I trusted had deceiv'd,
  And those I lov'd had me forsaken ;
Again in rapturous dreams I lived,
  As by-gone feelings thou didst waken.

The sky grew crystal, as of yore,
   I saw far in the depths of heav'n ;
And angel-wings were glancing o'er
   Bright prospects to the future giv'n.

When low I saw thy father laid,
   And wept upon the turfless sod,
With bursting heart my steps delay'd ;
   There, breathing broken pray'rs to God,

I deem'd the day would never come
   When I should smile again on earth,
Or that my desolated home
   Would echo to the sounds of mirth.

Thou cam'st, and still thy gladd'ning pow'r
   Is felt through each succeeding day;
'Tis thou beguil'st the mournful hour
   With many a sportive, sweet assay

Of childish glee and love, o'erflowing
   In fond embraces and caresses ;
The fullness of thy heart bestowing
   As plays my hand among thy tresses.

And now with lofty aim I live,
   To guide thy guilelessness and youth,
And teach thy op'ning mind to strive
   For wisdom, virtue, honor, truth.

And earth is beautiful again,
   And lofty mount and rushing river,
And leafy bow'r and flow'ring plain,
   Speak in rich music-language ever ;

For love interprets ev'ry sound
  That comes upon the low wind sighing,
Or rises from the depths profound,
  With tones accordant still replying.

INDIAN HYMN TO THE MURKAWIS, BIRD OF THE GREAT SPIRIT.

WITH the deep'ning shades of the twilight hour
  Thou com'st, O bird! from thy world of bliss,
And to the still'd heart, with mystic pow'r,
  Thou speakest of things unknown in this.

Thou speakest of those to whom we are turning,
  Whose mem'ries we cherish with hope and with love,
To meet whom again the heart is still burning
  With a flame allied to the pure fires above.

Thou com'st in the twilight, when, solemn and sad,
  The glories of day are all veil'd from our view,
And in thy clear note, reverent, yet glad,
  We hear of the world of the good and the true.

They are there, they are there, the lov'd and departed,
  They wait for us there at the portals of day;
There shall they welcome us, the pure and true-hearted,
  What a vision of bliss! Away! let's away!

Bird of the Spirit ! thy note is still telling
  To hearts that are list'ning a tale of delight ;
Borne on the breezes, gently its swelling
  Solemnly comes o'er the silence of night.

Hark ! in that melody surely is breathing
  A message of love from the " shadowy band ;''
And in yon clouds are spirits receiving
  In the song of thy mate a tale of this land.

I see through the darkness their eyes brightly beaming,
  With a light like the moon when lonely she glides
Through the vault of deep blue, from whence there is
      streaming
  O'er the hush'd earth no radiance besides.

Bird of the Spirit, go tell the departed
  Fondly we cherish our faith ever true,
And wait in the spirit-land with the pure-hearted,
  In bowers of bliss our love to renew.

REVERIE ASCENDING ROCKFISH GAP, ALLEGHANY MOUNTAINS, VA.

MOONLIGHT on the mountains ! and as we upward rise,
Floods of soft'ning radiance are falling from the skies ;
Each rugged rock and pinnacle in the shadowy gleam
With warrior bold and sachem wise thickly peopled
    seem ;

And from every cleft and deeply shaded dell
Come forth patriot spirits there that through sunlight
    dwell ;
They claim their native land, there wander through
    the night,
There perform the festal dance, or in the chase delight ;
They lead the life again they led in days of yore,
Ere o'er the waters wide the dread pale-face came o'er.
Beneath yon aged tree, that casts its shade around,
A warrior and a maiden are seated on the ground ;
The neyhom's varied plumage enwraps his noble form,
His diadem's of the eagle's plume that soars above the
    storm.
His thoughts are not of love, the heaving of his breast
Tells some weight of sorrow disturbs his spirit's rest ;
His looks are sad and mournful, his eyes are downward
    cast,
As he ponders on the present and on the sadden'd past.
He sees the ancient forest cast wide its shelt'ring shade,
He hears returning footsteps come through the forest
    glade ;
Quick bounding to his view a warrior bold appears,
And to meet his greeting a trophy proudly rears.
Remembrance warms within him as from a trance he
    wakes,
And, kindling with a patriot's fire, in indignation
    speaks.
As by a leader rallied, shades thickly gather round,
Every shrub and mossy stone a habitant has found.
They list with mute attention and fix'd, serious thought:
The injuries of their wronged race are before them
    brought.

They remember when the pale-face, a helpless stranger,
    came :
They nourish'd him with garner'd corn and with
    hunted game.
They led him to their wigwams, they cheer'd him
    with their fire,
They bade him welcome to their feasts, and confidence
    inspire.
For him they raised the battle-cry and broke the string
    in twain ;
For him they ceas'd the strife, and smok'd the calumet
    again.
They hail'd him as a brother, they lov'd him as a
    friend,
And with their firm affection higher feelings blend.
But when the stranger pale-face powerful became,
He forgot their kindness, and wrapp'd their towns in
    flame ;
With increasing pow'r oppressing, he swept them from
    the earth,
And the craving of their heritage to numerous ills gave
    birth.
Now the remnant wander, a scatter'd, broken band,
Far from their fathers' graves and their native land.
The arts of peace they know not, their sylvan sports
    denied,
How many of their brethren in misery have died !
The accursed fire-water so abject them has made,
Oft they beg a boon of those who have their rights
    betray'd.
Will the Great Spirit never his children more befriend?
Unto their hard oppressors will he no demon send?

Will no dread Manitou arise in clouds of wrath,
And hurl the lightning of his ire upon their guilty
　　path?
Shall not blood cry forth from vale and mountain
　　height?
Shall not our sighs ascend duly as morning light
Mantles in glory the broad lands he to our fathers gave,
And which the ruthless white man's hand has made a
　　nation's grave?
The list'ning circle heard, and the war-whoop's savage
　　cry
Broke the silence of the night, appealing to the sky;
The spirit-shout was echoed from mount and sylvan
　　glen,
And the shadowy band slow glided from the haunts of
　　men.

A ROSE BLOOMING LATE IN AUTUMN.

Rose, fair rose! why dost thou bloom
　　So lonely here? The garden's drear,
And thou dost give thy sweet perfume
　　But to the unconscious air.

Veil, then, thy bloom, and guard thy sweets
　　Till the bright hours of spring,
For now thy blush no Philomela greets,
　　Nor at thy closing hour thy dirge will sing.

MY OWN WORLD.

I LIVE in a dear little world of my own,
Where hope ever smiles and griefs never come ;
And vines are enwreathing my own little bow'r,
That blossom and bud and are ever in flow'r.

When the wind whistles low and bright stars are
    shining,
'Mong roses and myrtles I soft lay reclining,
And phantoms of bliss around me then hover,
And, smiling, comes joy, and dimpled all over.

When the moon looks down through the leaves of the
    trees,
And the sweet breath of zephyr comes on the breeze,
Such whisp'rings of music steal through my bower,
As lightly it wooes the buds and the flow'r.

I dream that bright spirits from some far sphere
Have come in their love to visit me here ;
My soul bursts its fetters and throws off its care,
To hold in the converse of spirits a share.

When morning, bright-gemm'd, through the gray dawn
    is stealing,
And the slumber of birds and of flow'rs is unsealing ;
When the ripple of waters runs sparkling and clear,
And fresh opens the rose in the coppice-wood near ;

My spirit goes forth all joyous and bright,
While the glory of day, in its splendor of light,
Bears it onward and on through the blue vault of heav'n,
Till it joins the mild hours that herald the even.

Then softly it seeks the horizon's pale verge,
Where Venus, soft pillow'd, reclines on the surge,
And, nestling 'mid rose-tints and dew-gems till dawn,
Rises buoyant and fresh with the bright coming morn.

THE OCEAN.

SUBLIMEST of creation's forms,
In sunlit calms or dark'ning storms;
When peaceful spreads thy azure breast,
An emblem of unbroken rest;
When wavelets lift their crests of white,
With graceful heave in glowing light,
Or in wild commotion tost,
Impetuous, from coast to coast,
Deep calleth unto deep again,
Through all the wide and surging main,
And at their hollow voices rise
The waves unto the stormy skies.
No sound is heard but their deep roar
Along the rock-ribb'd solemn shore,
As fearfully their manes are tost,
Defying bold the rocky coast;

Or, sportively, they throw on high
Their spray unto the azure sky,
Like feathery curl of ostrich plumes,
Like showers of pearly petal'd blooms,
Like snow-flakes floating through the air,
So bright, so glist'ning, pure, and fair;
Till, by degrees, the waves subside,
And billows gently billows chide;
And less impetuous is the surge,
Less wild the wailing of the dirge
That, coming o'er thy heaving path,
Gives utt'rance to thy stormy wrath,
Till, soft as song from infancy,
Come murmurs from the shore to thee,
And calm as lakelet thou dost lie
Beneath the deep blue of the sky.
No ripple on thy glassy breast
Forebodes the hour of thy unrest,
But forms of birds in the mid-air
Distinctly are reflected there:
The halcyon, harbinger of rest,
Floats brooding on her wat'ry nest;
Thy various tribes, in joyous sport,
The sunshine in their pastimes court;
The nautilus spreads out her sail,
As if to woo a loit'ring gale;
The huge leviathans of the deep
A festal on thy surface keep,
And in their pride of strength, away,
Where heav'n and sea commingling lay,
With wanton pow'r assert their reign
O'er the undivided main,

Nor brook that the curious eye
Too near their wondrous forms espy.
   It is in vain we would essay
To tell of what thou dost display.
We feel thy grand sublimity;
We feel thy dread infinity;
We feel that thou an emblem art
Of Eternity, of which we're part,—
An emblem of eventful life,
Its calms, vicissitudes, and strife;
An emblem, in thy fearful wrath,
Of an unfetter'd demon's path;
An emblem of beneficence,
Of grandeur and omnipotence.
   Weak are all words, and undefin'd,
To give thy impression on the mind.
Whether with delight on thee we gaze
Beneath the mild moon's silver rays,
Or when the sun's effulgence throws
Its radiance on thy hush'd repose,
Or stars look down, and, mirror'd there,
See another heav'n as fair
As that in which benignity
Has shrined their bright divinity;
Or winds call to thee from afar,
And wake the elemental war,
And thou, arising in thy might,
Wild, billow'd, rushing to the fight,
Liftest thy fearful waves on high,
In wrath commingling with the sky.
   Weak are all words, yet still we burn
With love of thee, and often turn
Along the smooth beach sanded way,

At evening's pensive hour, to stray,
And watch the sun's broad, glowing rim
Sink 'neath thy waves, as the vesper hymn
Awakes in varied minstrelsy
To Him who form'd thee, glorious sea!
And when the morning's ruddy glow,
Reflected in thy waves below,
A golden radiance o'er thee throws,
And in thy depths serenely glows,
Our souls, on the wings of morn,
O'er thy immensity are borne,
And thoughts awake, thou circled sea,
Of the shoreless waves of eternity.

    Whatever aspect thou dost wear,
Still thou art fearful, grand, or fair;
Still thou dost musings high awake,
Whether thy waters gently break
In ripples on the shell-strown sand,
Or where the rock-protected land
Throws back thy spray with sullen pride,
Or thou their puny force deride,
With sudden leap o'er crag and rock,
Convulses earth with thy rude shock,
And as a genie in his play,
Tosses on high the drenching spray,
And sends with the wild wind shrill
Thy voice to glade and echoing hill;
Or in murmurs soft and clear
Steals upon the list'ning ear,
To troubled bosoms giving balm,
And to the weary whispering calm,
Infusing, in thy immensity,
Forgetfulness of self in thee.

THE RETROSPECT.

I.

Whilst the rude boreal through inclement skies
　　Drove his vast stores of rain and hail and sleet,
With careless heart and ever-eager eyes
　　We wandered on, with often-loit'ring feet.
Where the blue sea in peaceful beauty lies,
　　Temp'ring the breath that breathes on fruit and grain,
In southern France and 'neath Italian skies,
　　Where Ceres' and where Flora's lengthened reign
　　Throughout the year their fruitful sway maintain.

II.

Nurturing tall olive-trees on Cannes' shore,
　　The lofty palm on Genoa's sunny bay,
The orange and the citron's golden store,
　　Where Mentone, lovely as an Eden, lay,
With craggy heights and fearful, dizzy steep,
　　Above the voyager of the mountain way;
While, far below, the surging of the deep
　　Told of the dangers that beneath him lay,
　　Where the bright waters sparkle in their play.

III.

Where the wild Apennines, as tempest tost,
　　Raging and chafing in their stormy wrath,

All suddenly transfixed, their motion lost,
　　Bearing the impress of a genie's path ;
While oft between, full many a lovely glen,
　　With terrac'd hill and neatly-trellis'd vine,
And chestnuts waving round the haunts of men,
　　And growing grain, and olives, in the shine
　　Of the warm sun, where to the south the slopes decline,

IV.

Invited tarriance in romantic nook,
　　To feast the heart with nature's loveliness ;
On varied scenes of grandeur there to look,
　　And garner stores, life's future years to bless ;
To many a sacred fane of ancient days,
　　To many a palace of a princely line,
Through whose rude rents the wild wind, sportive,
　　　　plays
　　With the slight tendrils of the mantling vine,
　　Whose purple fruit and polish'd leaves entwine

V.

Round broken arch and ruin'd portal proud,
　　As if maternal nature gently sought
From mocking eyes their fallen grace to shroud,
　　And teach a lore with heav'nly wisdom fraught ;
Though here, regardless of her pious care,
　　Unhallow'd pow'r oppresses with his sway
Those who her bounteous gifts should equal share,
　　Till bow'd with toil, to meagre want a prey,
　　Unconscious of their rights, they servilely obey.

VI.

There children beautiful as poet's dream,
 Models of painters' and of sculptors' art,
In marble pure and on the canvas seem
 Of life and immortality a part.
Nursed in such scenes, and 'neath such glowing skies,
 Lo, Titian's, and lo, Raphael's magic art,
And Guido's pencil, breathing harmonies,
 As with an inspiration touch the heart,
 And gleams of heav'n to the soul impart.

VII.

See where Aurora to the sleeping earth
 Unbars the portals of the glowing dawn,
Gemming with dews, and waking tuneful mirth,
 As unto renovated life the world is born;
While in his chariot the yet dusky day
 On rolling clouds by fiery coursers borne,
Chafing, impatient of the hour's delay,
 That at the eastern gate hails their return,
 When the receding night seeks his accustom'd bourne.

VIII.

Around his car the circling sisters press,
 With elastic steps, the joyous hours of morn;
Beyond the advancing noontide fervidness
 The mild herald of the eve moves on.
There promises of beauty and of joy appear,
 A happy day of deep, unclouded azure,
Such as is fabled where the golden year

Treads in the rosy path of thornless pleasure,
And soothing harmonies keep their unbroken measure.

IX.

But Time holds not such dance of joyance here,
 With fallen grandeur crumbling 'neath his sway,
Where cities to reviving learning dear
 Wear chaplets only of a former day;
And, sanctified by holy memories
 Of genius' toil and virtue's high emprise,
With mournful step the musing pilgrims press
 Upon the soil where buried greatness lies,
 With voice appealing to earth's destinies.

X.

Thou prostrate shrine, to which a world may come,
 Bearing the tribute of a grateful heart,
For light diffus'd first from thee that shone,
 When genius reawaken'd slumb'ring art;
When, as a phœnix from the smould'ring pyre,
 Shall conq'ring Freedom there unfold her wing,
Kindling in ardent hearts the sacred fire,
 And high resolve, in patriot breasts that spring,
 When Heav'n ordains, a nation off shall fling

XI.

The thraldom that has bound with iron chain
 To superstition and to despots' sway,
And, as one heart, throughout the wide domain
 United, file the galling links away.

Then thy blest sons, with equal rights endow'd,
   Shall see, beneath thy clear, cerulean skies,
Plenty, with commerce and with arts restor'd,
   And prosp'rous hamlets through thy valleys rise,
   Where crouching want in mis'ry's cell now lies.

XII.

Such thoughts as these pressed sadd'ning on the heart
   As on we wander'd, though oft with sense beguil'd,.
By nature's beauties and the works of art,
   'Midst poverty and want serene we smil'd,
Nor cast a furtive glance of warm desire
   Beyond the waters of the western main.
Blest in the luxury such climes inspire,
   Happy we breath'd the balm of fertile plain,
   Or climb'd the heights where winter holds his hoary
      reign.

XIII.

But when, in the rich valley of the Po,
   We saw the flow'rets of the spring appear,
And heard the blithe notes of the songster flow
   In warbled joy, melodious and clear,
Such thronging thoughts came o'er my waken'd breast
   Of home, and all its cherish'd inmates dear,
As one o'erwearied, I long'd to seek the rest
   Where glad, familiar faces greet and cheer,
   And bland affection smiles, throughout the year.

XIV.

Diffus'd through Nature are such sympathies,
   Waking responsive feelings to her lyre,

Whether she breathes of soothing harmonies,
　Or, in sublimer moods, the heart inspire
With musing high, her mastery she doth keep,
　And hath the pow'r to call up joy and tenderness
And fear from out their fountains deep,
　　And in the solitude with sights and sounds to bless,
　That chase away all thoughts of loneliness;

XV.

Inspiring with hope and love and trust
　In the pervading Pow'r that all sustains,
Calling, with renovated bloom, the flow'rs from dust,
　And filling with their vital juice the veins
Of leafless branch, of shrub and lofty tree,
　Till beauty clothe their naked forms again,
And Nature, rob'd as for a jubilee,
　All lovely shows on mountain and on plain,
　And a rejoicing voice is heard through her domain.

XVI.

Then, as I stood in that soft clime serene,
　And pluck'd the native wild flow'r from its stem,
My heart, responsive, answer'd to the scene,
　And this the simple song I sung to them.
And the lov'd images, that I had stor'd
　From childhood in the secret of my heart,
Came, as prompt vassals of magician's word,
　From far-off realms, obsequious to his art,
　Unto that hour their ministry to impart.

Oh, no, I do not dwell alone,
I am not lonely now;

My spirit gives an answ'ring tone
    To the waving of the bough,—

To the carol of the bird,
    To the gushing of the spring,
To the slightest leaf that's stirr'd,
    To every living thing.

To the ocean tempest tost,
    To its smooth, mirror'd calm,
To its murm'ring on the coast,
    To its mighty pow'r of harm.

To the mountain's lofty height,
    That boldly meets the sky;
To the vales that laugh in light,
    Where crystal fountains lie.

To the gray of solemn dawn,
    O'er the silence of the sea;
To the gladness of the morn,
    When it breaks forth gloriously.

To the clouds swift floating by,
    To the deep-blue vault of heav'n,
To the sunset-tinted sky,
    To the tempest through it riven.

To the stars far holy light;
    To the sun's meridian blaze;
To the mysteries of night;
    To the moon's subduing rays.

These sympathies of mine
Developed more shall be,
As I kneel at heaven's shrine,
Through all eternity.

XVII.

Now leave we Italy's benignant skies,
  Her classic streams, and fields of patriot fame,
And enter where the Switzer's country lies,
  Whose hardy sons the rights of freemen claim ;
And 'mong their verdant vales and snowy peaks
  Hear in the tones of every passing wind
A voice, that in awak'ning accents speaks
  Unto the love of freedom in the mind,
  And hatred of enslaving bonds that bind

XVIII.

Man to his brother man in durance vile,
  And in a world where streams of gladness flow,
And goodness ever bounteous sheds its smile,
  Extorts from bleeding hearts the sighs of woe.
Daughter of winds of heaven, and mountains high,
  Thou lov'st the lofty cliffs sublime to tread,
Robed in thy vestments tinted with the sky,
  With rainbow glories circling o'er thy head,
  And light effulgent round thy footsteps shed.

XIX.

Inspir'd by thee, thy sons have nobly bled,
  Sustaining with integrity of heart
The high resolve, and when thy steps have led
  To dungeons' drear, where many a dart

Of sorrow keen, and stern, oppressive pow'r,
　Cankers the soul, with renovating lay
Thou break'st upon the sadness of the hour,
　And glorious visions of a future day,
　With mild Religion heralding thy way

XX.

To far-off realms, where yet thy trumpet voice
　Hath ne'er been heard, enkindles in the soul
Fresh ardor high; and, trusting, they rejoice
　That, though a lapse of years away may roll,
The seed they've sown shall yet prolific spread,
　And a redundant harvest rich shall grow,
Though despots, with their with'ring step, may tread
　Their verdant fields progressively, though slow
　The disenthralling love of thee shall spread and glow.

XXI.

Superior to the sharp, subduing pain,
　The martyrs of the torture and the fire
In hymns of joy wake the exulting strain,
　And in an ecstasy of bliss expire;
For that the noble effort shall not die,
　Freedom of conscience and of law to give,
But their devotion unto promptings high,
　In blessings rich to future times shall live,
　And clear away the mists that now deceive.

XXII.

Then, Switzerland, upon thy brow shall be
　A stain of dark'ning shame, that thou,

Lover of freedom and among the free,
　Should lend thy sons, obsequious to bow
Round kingly thrones, and guardian there to wait,
　The ministers of their will, to bind
Souls that, with aspiring hopes elate,
　Would rend away time-hallowed wrongs that blind,
　And light and knowledge give unto mankind.

XXIII.

But lovely are thy green, sequestered vales,
　Thy rushing torrents and thy woods of pine,
Thy clustered hamlets, where the storm-cloud sails,
　As eyrie built, upon thy cliffs recline.
And there the daring lovers of the chase,
　As wind upborne, elastic bound along,
With eager joy appalling dangers face,
　And buoy their spirits up with many a song,
　Echoed with answ'ring tone the secret glens among.

XXIV.

And clearer in thy sky the depths of blue,
　More dazzling there the mountain's robe of white;
More lovely is its sunset-tinted hue
　When glowing in the evening's purple light.
Serene above the moon more brightly shines,
　As if reflected there she loves to be;
With ling'ring beam upon the height reclines,
　Enamored of the spotless purity
　Of that unheaving, ever-silent sea.

XXV.

Whoe'er hath looked upon those heights sublime,
    Where man's aspiring step hath never trod,
And on the beauty of many a deep ravine,
    Where grateful nature only worships God,
Shall feel within his secret bosom grow
    A sense of awe he ne'er before hath owned,
And pride-subduing shall the feeling glow
    While gazing on those cliffs so purely zon'd,
    Where solitude with grandeur sits enthron'd.

XXVI.

Man's marring hand hath left no traces there
    Upon those heights from central earth upheav'd ;
As he inhales the soul-inspiring air,
    There seems a song of joy around him breath'd ;
Nature's sweet hymn, from vale and lofty height,
    As from pure altars, offer'd to the skies.
Where fall the shades, and where the glow of light,
    Where the vast solitude in beauty lies,
    In chorus sweet the grateful voices rise,

XXVII.

Hymning of the creation's dawning birth,
    When chaos felt light's vivifying glow,
Till beauty cloth'd the face of dædal earth,
    And streams majestic through its bosom flow,
And oceans heav'd, and mountains lofty rose,
    Rob'd with the verdure of the first young spring,
And the fair scenes that still it doth disclose,
    Though Time unceasingly has sped his wing,
    No sad decay he to her charms doth bring.

HYMN OF NATURE.

FIRST rose the choral hymn
　　From young creation's breast,
Whilst the glory yet was dim
　　On the earth in her unrest.

As the light's first golden beaming
　　Divided chaos' floating shroud,
And, in faint radiance streaming,
　　Tinted morning's orient cloud.

As the waveless face of ocean
　　First undulating heav'd,
And from interchanging motion
　　Its grandeur dread receiv'd.

As the firm-rooted mountains,
　　With forests girdled round,
Sent forth their many fountains
　　To fertilize the ground.

As the first vernal springing
　　Of herb and tree and flow'r,
Their scents and hues were bringing
　　To earth a beauteous dow'r.

As the mighty rivers flowing
    Their barriers burst away,
With reflected light now glowing,
    In caves now hid from day.

Thy mountains now are hoary,
    High pinnacled with snow,
But unblemish'd is thy glory;
    Thou tell'st no tale of woe.

Thou pæans still dost hymn
    From many an holy altar;
Thy beauty grows not dim,
    Nor thy many-ton'd voice falter.

But, in harmonious symphony,
    As at creation's dawn,
Ascends unto the Deity
    Praise as on that glad morn.

PORT PELLIS CASTLE.

When conqu'ring Cæsar with his legions came
    From Rome imperial to this savage isle,
And brave hearts quail'd before his mighty name,
    'Mong wond'ring men he built this mould'ring pile.

Dense was the forest of the oaken shade,
   Where Druids their unholy rites observ'd,
And men submissive through their dark arts made,
   By superstition sway'd, obedient serv'd.

Next rose the pagan temple's beauteous fane,
   To less remorseless gods implor'd in pray'r,
With off'rings unto Jove's or Juno's name,
   And incense flung upon the ambient air.

These passed away as Time's unwearied wing,
   In flight progressive still his shadow threw,
And from the east advancing, the day-spring
   Of light eternal here its votaries drew.

And see where now in consecrated ground
   They lay a brother in the parent dust,
With weeping friends in solemn circle round,
   Soothing their grief with holy hope and trust.

Upon the precincts of that humble grave
   With rev'rent heart the solemn words are said,
Recording a Redeemer's pow'r to save,
   E'en from the gloomy mansions of the dead.

The Druid's most unholy creed of fear,
   The pagan's ritual of pomp and pride,
Propos'd no balm of healing unction here
   To the survivors when their lov'd ones died.

And lo! around the grateful fruits that spring
   From the meek faith by holy martyrs spread,
Where brooded rav'ning passion's baleful wing,
   Hope and charity their influence shed.

In the soft light of the receding day
　　Green fields and cottages all peaceful lie,
And calm and beautiful the outspread bay
　　Reflects the tinted glories of the sky.

'Mid clust'ring vines and sweet flow'rs blossoming,
　　And grassy plots and broad, o'ershadowing tree,
Refresh'd by gentle Zephyr's fanning wing,
　　As soft he floats o'er the cerulean sea,

Stand many a cot where virtue and where love
　　An earthly paradise of joy have made,
Sweet as was feign'd in fair Arcadian grove,
　　Where dulcet sounds time's rapid flight delay'd.

Oh, blessed faith ! still may thy influence spread,
　　Till circled earth bows to thy holy sway;
On hearts renew'd still may thy grace be shed,
　　Till ev'ry impulse its pure laws obey.

CARISBROOKE.

Thou fair, sweet valley, with thy silv'ry stream,
Lovely as fairy-land or fairy's dream !
Look'd not the monarch from his castled keep
When thou in soft moonlight didst peaceful sleep,
And long'd the peasant's deep repose to share,
Who knows no ills but those of toil and care,
To tear the diadem from his royal brow,
And live in joys that humble states allow,

With wife and children in some cottage blest,
Far from ambition's strifes that courts molest,
Nurt'ring the seeds of virtue and of love,
That win a crown of amaranth above?

LINES SUGGESTED BY THE APPEAR-ANCE OF THOSE EMPLOYED IN THE FACTORIES.

WITH weary feet and aching head,
   And hearts that scarcely know delight,
Still in the same dull round they tread
   From weary morn till weary night.

Children of toil and poverty,
   The common air and sun of heav'n,
That to the herds and flocks are free,
   To their heart-longings are not giv'n.

But, penn'd within unwholesome walls,
   The hue of health deserts their cheeks,
And nature's importuning calls
   In vain through failing nature speaks.

Shall they who plead in Afric's cause,
   Till hard oppressors loos'd their prey,
Neglect toward these those Christian laws
   That others, taught by them, obey?

KENILWORTH.

OH, Amy! of thy loveliness, thy beauty, and thy
    grace,
In vain we seek 'mong these rent walls a vestige now to
    trace ;
But still our fancy loves to dwell where'er thou mightst
    have trod,
With many thoughts of love and thee we press the ver-
    dant sod,
And think how oft the trusting heart to sorrow is be-
    tray'd
In the Eden that a young idolatry has made,
And tears of pity at thy fate are gath'ring in the eye,
That thou, sweet flow'r, crush'd in thy bloom, so soon
    wast doom'd to die.

THE HIGHLAND CHIEFTAIN'S BRIDE.

To me he spoke no words of love,
    But spoke in tones of voice that melt ;
And well I saw in his dark eye
    How deep the feeling that he felt.

But, ah! I knew o'er land and sea
  He'd wander far for many a year,
And wearily, in solitude,
  I fear'd to shed the bitter tear.

For, oh! a rover bold was he,
  And ev'ry peril had a charm
To lure him from a quiet home,
  And seek for danger and alarm.

And well I thought to guard my heart,
  And seek in love a mate less bold,
And, in a humble cottage home,
  A life of peaceful joy to hold.

But, ah! full many songs he sung
  Of triumph high and mirthful glee,
When dangers great had been o'ercome
  By daring bold on land and sea.

And round the roving chieftain's bride
  He spread a charm undream'd before:
With him the mountain high to climb,
  And sail with him the rock-bound shore.

And now, a happy bride, I dwell
  By turns with him on land and sea;
And, trusting in his fost'ring love,
  I careless rove, from sorrow free.

  *   *   *   *   *

When border minstrelsy was gayly sung
   To plumed chief within each feudal hold,
To words like these the hoary minstrel strung
   His harp, to lady fair and baron bold.

But now, amid the heather waving high,
   No more is seen the plume, nor pibroch shrill
Wakes its wild notes where the fierce battle-cry
   Answer'd to beacon-blaze from hill to hill.

Where armed ranks, in war's proud array,
   With pennon floating to the mountain breeze,
And measur'd step, mov'd to the battle fray,
   The hand of labor rears umbrageous trees.

Upon the lonely moor the humble cot
   A hardy race send forth, inur'd to toil;
Frugal their board, penurious their lot,
   For scant their portion from the yielding soil.

But 'neath the wing of Peace the virtues grow,—
   Patient endurance, kindness to their race;
On many a rugged brow the glow
   Of honest worth lights up a manly grace.

And happier far the peaceful eve and morn
   Than when the tumult of the battle-cry
Awoke the sleepers, ere the tints of dawn
   Streak'd with bright gleams the gloaming eastern
      sky.

More happy fruits our holy faith shall give,
　As its blest teachings sway the human heart ;
As men submissive to its dictates live,
　Joy shall increase and misery depart.

TO A YEW BEFORE THE LIBRARY WINDOW AT ABBOTSFORD.

Thou melancholy yew,
　To churchyard consecrate,
Water'd with tears as dew,　　　.
　Why near this hall of state ?

Mask, revelry, and sportive mirth
　Might here have held their jubilee:
Thou mourner o'er insensate earth,
　What are such things to thee ?

The mighty of the earth
　Here bow'd before the sway of mind,
And sons of peasant birth
　Homage of heart and love assign'd.

What, then, O mournful yew!
　Dost thou before this hall of state?
Thy garb of sombre hue
　Is to churchyard consecrate.

Prophetic wast thou planted here,
    In prescience of dark days?
In the glow of a sun's career,
    To warn of shadow'd rays?

Of the light of the spirit flown?
    Of the heart's cherish'd dead?
Of life's bright visions gone,
    Low laid in sorrow's bed?

———————

TO THE HAWTHORN PLANTED BY QUEEN MARY AT LOCH LEVEN.

THOU solace of unhappy Scotia's queen,
    Still blooming with the mournful wall-flow'r round!
Thou fair memento, in this gloomy scene,
    Of her who here a transient prison found!

She planted thee when loneliness and grief
    Dimm'd the bright lustre of her hazel eye;
And, nurt'ring thee, perchance she found relief
    To bitter thoughts that prompt the frequent sigh.

The massive castle-walls in ruin lie,
    The wind sad music makes through the worn pile;
But thou dost lift thy blossoms to the sky,
    And with thy fragrance passing steps beguile,
Admonishing the gazer's eye and thought
That purity and love in Mary's bosom wrought.

THE CELL OF TASSO.

FERRARA'S streets are silent now,
  The voice of revelry and mirth
And pageantry, to which men bow,
  Have pass'd away from earth.

Vain is the promise flatt'ring pride may lend,
  Of glorious immortality and fame,
To those who with their proud pretensions blend
  No gifts of mind, nor deeds of virtuous name.

Awhile may tinsel, pomp, and power supply
  Themes for the vulgar mind to laud and praise;
But deeds of merit, and of emprise high,
  Alone a lasting monument can raise.

The costly tomb, the sepulchre of kings,
  The ancient line, the heraldry of pride,
And all that from a vain ambition springs,
  As a vain pageantry have liv'd and died.

And oft with careless footstep now is trod
  Where the proud palace rear'd its marble wall,
Whose blinded princes, impotent for good,
  Were bound in vain ambition's thrall.

But that one spot, however poor or mean,
    Where virtuous Genius mourn'd, or joy'd, or wrought,
Is cherished as an ever-sacred scene,
    And with deep reverence by the gifted sought.

Therefore, Ferrara, is that gloomy cell,
    Close, low and dark, by pilgrims often sought,
Where, in hard durance, Tasso once did dwell
    For imputed madness, by Love's passion wrought.

The sun's bright rays could scarcely there descend
    To bless the vision of his upturned eye,
Nor the fresh air with the heav'd sigh blend,
    As rose his prayer in fervor to the sky.

How panted then his spirit to be free,
    For dew-gemm'd flow'r, and glittering mountain
        height,
For winding stream, and woodland minstrelsy,
    For shade at noon, and solemn star at night!

Yet oft, perchance, 'mid his desponding hours,
    His genius to his drooping spirit came,
Blest solacer, from fair Elysian bow'rs,
    With radiant wing and glowing eyes of flame.

And all unfetter'd, in the holy trance,
    Bright visions pass'd before his unfilm'd eye;
He felt his spirits in the pure air dance;
    He trod the sparkling firmament on high.

Deeply he drank such rapturous delight
  As gifted bards in their high lays inspire;
And still ascending heav'nward in his flight,
  Touch'd his pure lips with Heav'n's altar fire.

'Tis thus no bars can fetter Genius' power,
  Nor bonds confine to its abode of clay;
But, immateriality its dower,
  Through space domain it freely wings away.

And through all time to it the influence giv'n
  The spirits to arouse of darken'd men;
To chosen sons the special gift of heav'n,
  'Tis theirs the light to reillume in them.

Therefore we hail with sympathetic breast
  Where'er the footsteps of the great have been,
And with deep rev'rence press the spot where rest
  The forms that held the godlike guest within.

OLIVE-TREES.

On the ledges of the mountains, in small plots of earth, said to have been carried thither by the peasants, are olive-trees growing; the plots are many of them so small as to hold but one tree.

Thou pale-leav'd tree !
Emblem of peace and fruitfulness,
  Thou growest on the mountain-side,
  Where no small streamlets rippling glide,
And all around is barrenness.

 Yet thou a harvest rich doth yield
To the poor peasant of the glen,
  Who, with their humble lot content,
  Seek naught beyond their world so pent,
Far from the haunts of lordly men.

 Emblem of peace ! thou minist'rest to them ;
Their wishes and their wants are few,
  And thy dark fruit from the laden bough
  They pluck with many a fervent vow,
Grateful that heav'n doth thus its gifts renew.

 Oh, ye who dwell where Nature's lavish waste
Scatters her varied gifts profusely round,
  Where the fruit-bearing flowers,
  Matur'd with sun and showers,
Yield plenteous harvests from the teeming ground,

Go to the mountain-homes,
To the poor hamlet, thinly scatter'd far,
   Where nature's barrenness
   Makes scenes of dreariness,
And bless the favoring star

That plac'd you where the fertile mead
Gives its full treasures to the lab'ring hind,
   And odors sweet from flowers,
   And vine-encircl'd bowers,
Come on each passing wind.

CRADLE SONG OF EVIL GENII.

LULLABY, lullaby, wild winds are blowing;
Lullaby, lullaby, wild waves are flowing.
We nurse thee in storm, when the dire tempest's wrath
Scatters destruction and blight in its path.

Lullaby, lullaby, thy cradle's the pine;
Here, 'mong its waving boughs, fearless recline.
Thy dreams are vague flittings of ambition and scorn,
The germs of a hero now in thy soul dawn.

Lullaby, lullaby, we've ta'en thee away
From thy parents of earth, whose hearts are of clay.
We'll inweave in thy frame such passions of fire
As with deeds dark and dread thy soul shall inspire.

From obscurity dim thou shalt 'merge to the world.
When thy banner of terror thou wide hast unfurl'd
Men shall hail thee a god, and in thy path
Follow on, at thy call, on missions of wrath.

Lullaby, lullaby, our soul doth rejoice,
The deeds of thy manhood shall echo our voice;
In thy cradled slumbers we hail thee our child,
Nurtur'd for daring, dark, fearful, and wild.

'Mid this savage silence, by the vulture's scream broke,
Where hid volcanic fires mutter sulphurous smoke,
We hail thee our child, our minister of wrath,
And with the meteor's glare we'll lighten thy path.

BATAILLE.

In Lake Maggiore are three islands. On one of them—entirely
formed by art, and called, for its pre-eminent beauty, La Isola Bella
—is a large palace and garden. Upon one of the trees is still seen,
carved in the rind, " Bataille!" said to have been cut by Bonaparte
the evening previous to the battle of Marengo.

UNDER the shadow of the branches green,
    Amid La Bella Island's garden ground,
In the soft twilight, one of regal mien
    Stood where the choicest flow'rets bloom around.
Gently the dews from fair Italia's skies
    Refreshing fall on ev'ry leaf and flow'r,

And the sweet vesper songs of birds arise,
  In accordance with the twilight soothing hour.
Incense from earth arose, and one might deem,
  So gently stole the wavelet to the shore,
So tranquillizing was the fair lake scene,
  Its influence would the love of peace restore.
With sunset glory ting'd, in grandeur rose
  Such scenes as Italy in pride may show,
On which the eye, delighted, will repose,
  E'en when the heart, grief-stricken, sinks in woe.
He stood in pride beneath that verdant tree,
  Ambition o'er his heart held stern control ;
The master of the world he dream'd to be,
  And war's unhallow'd passion fired his soul.
In the deep stillness of that holy hour
  The trumpet and the clarion shrill he hears,
And all the victor's pageantry of pow'r,
  To lure him on, before his mind appears.
Blazon'd in glory, lo ! Marengo's fame,
  Though trac'd in characters by blood distain'd,
To future times shall consecrate his name,
  A nation's hero, by France proudly claim'd.

The orphan's cry, the widow's bitter tear,
  The carnage and the wounds on battle-field,
The burning village, and the hearth-stone drear,
  To these, say, would the warrior's purpose yield ?
The laurel chaplet circles round his head,
  Above the slaught'ring cry the loud acclaim he
      hears;
Incense is breath'd, and, at his haughty tread,
  The conquer'd quail, the conqu'rors greet with
      cheers.

Thy holy beauty, Nature, on his breast
  Exerts in vain its soft, appealing smile ;
And, 'midst the scenes by thee most fondly blest,
  Unheeding of thy charms, he carves " Bataille ! "

THE WIZARD'S DEATH.

THE wizard lay in his charméd cave,
By the mountain-torrent's rushing wave,
  And short the breath he drew.
He cast to the future an anguish'd eye,
And thought of the past with a bitter sigh,
  For well his fate he knew.

The compact in health and youth he seal'd,
By which to him was the pow'r reveal'd
  To gain each wish'd-for end,
Had ceas'd to exist, and the forfeit now
He saw with a scorch'd and writhing brow :
  The corse was the soul to attend !

And, throughout all its future destiny,
From its companion 'twas ne'er to be free ;
  And its aim was still to cross,
With the promptings of a low desire,
That first was lit at an earthly fire,
  To the soul's eternal loss.

And now the dæmon o'er him stood,
With a grim delight to see his mood,
  And relentings knew he none.
As the spirit pass'd from the wasted mould,
Contortions dire and shiverings cold
  Convuls'd, and the soul was gone.

Then the howling wind did lift
From the snowy mountain-clift
  A mantle so white and cold;
And, with that shroud,
Bound in a cloud
  The corse so haggard and old.

The cloud pass'd over the stormy sea,
And the caves where his grammery
  Had conjured up phantoms of fear;
O'er the yawning cleft,
By the earthquake reft,
  And the desert so lonely and drear.

O'er the burning crater it hover'd awhile,
And the corse look'd down with a ghastly smile,
  To see its future home.
For, though he felt both terror and dread,
He scorn'd the shrive and penance said,
  And shouted, "I come! I come!"

Away through the regions of upper air,
Where the glorious stars were rolling fair,
  The cloud and corse then took their way;

11*

And through the vaults and depths of space
He read of ev'ry star the face,
   And tarried in Saturn's ray.

And the stricken soul was hov'ring yet,
With wail and rage and angry fret,
   That no beads were told and no pray'r was said;
For now the suff'ring spirit saw
Its sentence dread with grief and awe,
   And fain would its doom have fled.

But the cravings of sense were urgent still,
And the soul was bound to the body's will,
   As through this life's career;
Though from its companion 'twould fain have fled,
As it look'd with horror and shame and dread,
   And quak'd with grief and fear.

———————— .

THE MOUNTAIN.

SUBLIMELY grand thou lift'st thy head,
With thy pure robe upon thee spread,
The clear cerulean sky above,
Of hue such as the angels love,
While at thy base the flow'r-sprent green
Reflects a glow of emerald sheen.

From central earth thou look'st upheav'd,
The eternal snows around thee wreath'd,

As if to quench volcano fire,
That bade thee from the earth aspire,
And rais'd thy pinnacle on high,
Proud and cloud-cleaving, to the sky.

With solemn awe on thee we gaze,
And shrinkingly our eyes upraise;
For thou dost bear upon thy breast
The impress of a world's unrest,
When wild convulsions shook her frame,
And warring el'ments held their claim.

And now thou art no joyous thing;
The garland of the blooming spring
Doth ne'er upon thy bosom shed
Its perfume sweet, nor o'er thee spread
The lures that call the bird and bee,
Their minstrelsy to hymn to thee.

Thy gloomy glens the dark pines hold,
The waves of ice around them roll'd,
Unthaw'd by summer's genial hour,
Fit emblem is of despot's pow'r,
That yields not to affection's sway,
But coldly holds its cheerless way.

Silent thou art when summer's smile
Joyous tones from earth beguile;
When ev'ry green, waving bough
Seems whisp'ring to the air its vow,
When ev'ry little singing rill
Its benisons with mirth fulfill.

Along thy crags no joyous waves,
Nor gushing waters 'mong thy caves,
Nor sweet æolian harp is heard,
When Summer her soft air has stirr'd,
To steal through thy deserts wild,
Teaching nature's musing child.

But when the Spirit of the Storm
In clouds and mists enwrap thy form,
When lightnings hurtle round thy head,
And thunders peal in tones of dread,
Then wild wind unto wind doth call,
With moaning low at interval.

Sublime thou stand'st, a form of pow'r,
Attesting dread convulsion's hour;
But the rich vale beneath thee spread,
Where Ceres' choicest gifts are shed,
Our hearts with kindly feeling move,
And call forth gratitude and love.

THE LONELY CHILD.

"A child stood at the base of the mountain, motionless, with an expression on her face most sad and lonely, and eyes upturned earnestly gazing."

My life! it has no sunny spot,
  Save when I stand beside
Some crystal fountain's glassy face,
  And mark its waters glide,
Or in the shadow of the bloom
  Of some fair flow'ring tree.
Oh, then my spirit feels a thrill
  Of transient ecstasy.

I am a lonely, outcast child;
  I know no mother's care;
Upon my birth no mother smil'd,
  Nor father's earnest pray'r
Brought blessings on my infant head;
  For he was in his grave,
And my mother dwelt with pain and want
  Within the mountain-cave.

I mark the trav'ler wend his way
  Along the mountain-path,
And joy would spring in my young heart,
  But for me no eye he hath.

And then I look again to heav'n,
  And o'er the wide, wide earth,
And feel a stranger, all alone
  In the country of my birth.

The little birds their sweet song sing
  Upon the dancing spray,
The leaping water sparkling flows
  Light bounding on its way;
But still my heart one sorrow knows,
  From which it ne'er is free,—
Upon this bright and beauteous earth
  Alone, alone to be.

The heav'ns are bending clear above,
  The earth spreads out beneath,
I hear the hum of busy men
  Come with the evening's breath;
But word nor tone unto my ear
  With kindness ne'er is spoken.
Oh, how my soul would bless the sound
  Of love, to me a token!

To know that kind hearts heav'd a sigh
  Responsive unto mine;
To hear some clear, outspoken words
  Of sympathy divine.
Ah, then! a lone and sorrowing child
  No longer would I roam
Upon the solitary wild,
  But find with them a home.

DEATH OF THE NORSE KING.

Now onward, onward, gallant ship,
   Before the hurrying gale ;
O'er crested foam, through yawning gulf,
   Go thou with ready sail.

No earthly port thou seekest now,
   But one of warrior fame ;
Then proudly bear thee on thy way,
   Till thou art wrapt in flame.

For a king lies in thee, and a death
   Inglorious doth he fear,
Should he close his eyes on palace couch,
   And be borne on peaceful bier.

No valkyr for him then would wait,
   To bear to festive halls,
Where Odin with his heroes brave
   Sit in their cloud-girt walls.

But shame would be upon his soul,
   As he sought dark Hela's realm,
Denied an access to that heav'n
   She open'd unto them.

But should he in the flame expire,
   Between the sea and sky,
His soul would mount with the mounting fire
   To a destiny on high.

And warriors brave for him would wait
   At the festive palace halls,
And welcome to the genial feast
   Within the cloud-girt walls.

www.ingramcontent.com/pod-product-compliance
Lightning Source LLC
Chambersburg PA
CBHW030617270326
41927CB00007B/1208